Psychology II

Theories about genuine human being

By Dr. Edward Schellhammer

1st Edition in English, 2020, translated from the German Edition
© **Copyright 2020. Dr. Eduard Schellhammer. All rights reserved.**

ISBN-13: 9781478372103

www.SchellhammerBusinessSchool.com
www.SchellhammerInstitute.com

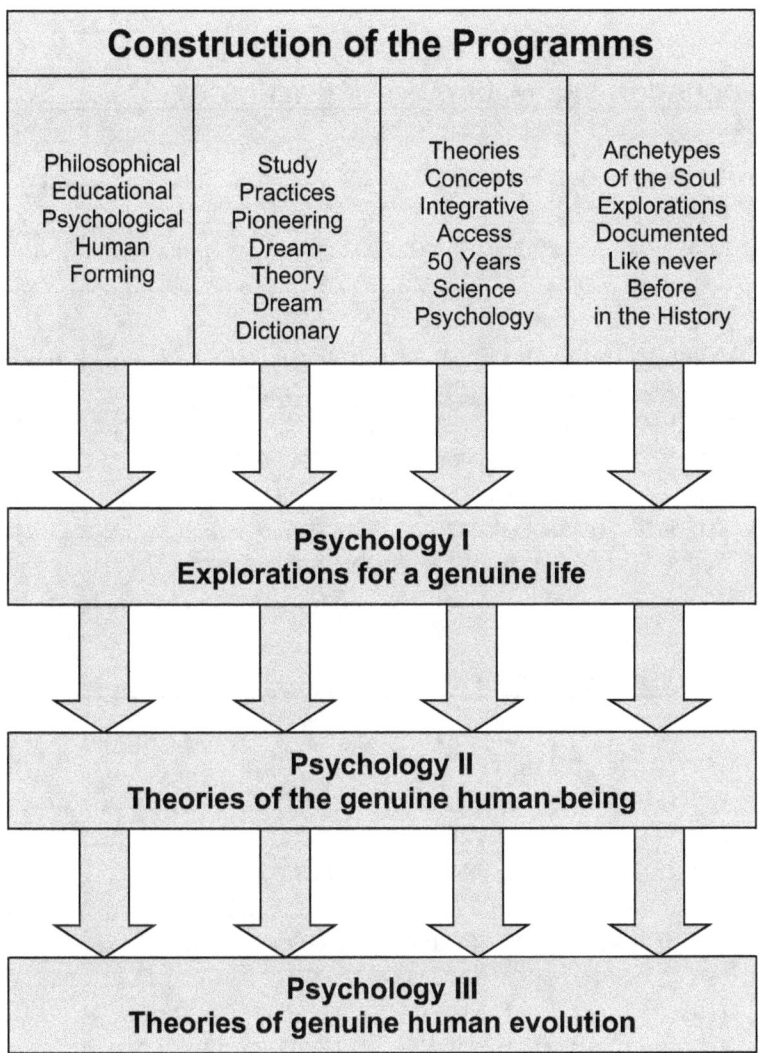

Construction of the Programms

Philosophical Educational Psychological Human Forming	Study Practices Pioneering Dream-Theory Dream Dictionary	Theories Concepts Integrative Access 50 Years Science Psychology	Archetypes Of the Soul Explorations Documented Like never Before in the History

Psychology I
Explorations for a genuine life

Psychology II
Theories of the genuine human-being

Psychology III
Theories of genuine human evolution

Table of Contents

List of Diagrams

In Somnis Veritas for Psychology II

In 'Somnis Veritas' has to do with the Psychology that explores the innermost 'mystery' of mankind. The 'Scientific' academic psychology does not and cannot explore these inner realities. academic psychology excludes everything that can only be explored and understood with the world of 'meaning' such as love, dreams, meditation, psychical energy, and the comprehensible and meaningful spirituality. A psychology that excludes the Archetypes of the Soul and with that the processes towards completeness and fulfillment is void of human value and hollow. Such an academic ('scientific') psychology is a scam and it fools the entire humanity.

Dreams tell the truth. Dreams are above theories, ideologies, and dogmas. During the last 33 years I had over 12,000 dreams about the state of humanity and the planet. I had an estimated 3000 dreams about humans' evolution and all processes of the Archetypes of the Soul.

Below are some examples:

A big assembly. I am talking. I reproach the people about how they did not take seriously what I said, not even the problems of the environment and what consequences we must expect. I explained, "Your children will have to live like they are in the Middle Ages, cholera included."

Scenes about a war in preparation like in the Middle Ages. Unbelievably perverse. They throw poor people into boiling water. They are the capitalists on highest level with their greed for gain.

An endless long earthquake, aesthetically devilishly beautiful. It is night. Fire and disruption are everywhere on the ground. Nobody wants to see this danger. The scenery extends to half of Europe. I can feel the ground trembling. I say to the people, "...!" But nobody listens to me.

I tell people, "I told you 20 years ago that the chemical composition (the chemical interactions) of all components .... (in the body) ...."

The ruler of the world is doing his work, everyday!

The rivers in the North are all about to overflow. They are frighteningly deep and with strong whirlpools and at an extremely dangerous speed. Nobody wants to see it.

They have placed a packet of dynamite in the town. One targeted shot and half of the earth explodes.

Many people are trying to cross a river. Most of them are drowning. This is because of the inability of the politicians to lead the people.

I can draw the sword of the king of the Grail from the rock and then I'm given an orb.

I see the Kings of the Grail sitting at the round table. They are discussing the grave lack of love, the disregard for psychical life, the lack of truth and the denial of the Spirit in the soul.

An expedition around the world which boils down to complete love is the most valuable thing that there is, and nobody has it anymore.

Within me is the temple of the Holy Grail. I know everything; I can reveal and help other people to experience this.

I have 'cosmic scissors' and with them I cannot only cut and separate, but also join and create wholeness. It is an enormous, very unfamiliar and alien gadget. I protest as I do not think they fit into my hand. But they do, they fit perfectly.

On the branch of a tree there sits an eagle with its wings spread, as if he wanted to show me the pattern of his wings. I take a closer look and discover that, on the one hand, it could be the image of king-archetype, but on the other hand it may be the living king of the Grail.

A king has got two pharaoh birds, very colorful and marvelously beautiful. It is said that these are magic birds. We come to the city of Jerusalem. I'm very glad we've finally reached the goal together with the kingly birds.

The truth and the Archetypes of the Soul are the primordial foundation and aim of science, human life, and society. Psychology doesn't have either! The entire social sciences do not have them. That is the scandalous drama of science!

The absence of the truth and of the Archetypes of the Soul produces enormous destructive energy and developments in sciences and societies.

It shows clearly that sciences do not take care of the archetypal, psychical, and spiritual evolution of mankind; nor do they have any respect for the creation.

Such science is a sham. Such sciences dehumanize the mind and soul and eliminate the dignity of humans.

Such sciences are infected with the most toxic virus ever to exist: the dynamic code for regicide and deicide. In the end, it will irreversibly and unstoppably lead to the doom.

It can happen within decades if drastic measures are not soon taken globally.

Dr. Eduard Schellhammer

Introduction: The Importance of Psychology

Psychology and the People

☐ Billions of people are greedy, lazy, stupid, and never want an all-embracing (national, global) renewal.

☐ Most humans are brainwashed, mentally poisoned and dehumanized: global or national renewal is not possible.

☐ The world is full of cowards, hypocrites, blabbers, false prophets, false politicians, false economists, and false priests.

☐ 6 billion people have deep inner pain and have lost faith (hope); they can't put trust into any 'renewal project'.

☐ People would go crazy and rebel if the right to drive a car or use an airplane would be severely limited.

☐ Most people are submissive to authorities. They trust and believe in them in an infantile psychical-spiritual way.

☐ People who want illusions, are driven by illusions, fantasies, magical thinking. They admire 'smoke and mirror' tactics.

☐ People tend to project weaknesses, bad and evil character, amoral doing and the devil in their own inner life onto other people.

☐ People project their longing for redemption and salvation onto authorities, state institutions and religion, or onto consumption.

☐ People do not want to elaborate their redemption and salvation through psychical-spiritual development.

☐ People think they are good, accepted, esteemed and valuable if they blindly obey others and institutions.

☐ Unconscious complexes of individuals are transmitted within the family to the next 3-4 generations.

☐ People are obsessed with having a home, car, partner (etc.) with the hope to gain salvation and happiness.

☐ Most people are 'human robots', irreparably deformed, misshaped and distorted since prenatal time.

☐ A lot of people are running or speculating for fast money with the least possible effort or performance.

☐ Too many unemployed people reject learning, hardworking, more working hours, or uncomfortable work.

☐ If the masses would dispose of much more money, they would only heat up stupid and blind consumption.

☐ A huge majority of people are not well educated and extremely ignorant and lazy for a real democracy.

☐ Most people greedily want much comfort, an easy life, fast results, cheap products, a lot of fun and distraction.

☐ To make oneself special with superficial self-presentation is more important than an integer character.

☐ The conceit to know what is fact, correct, just, right, and good (etc.) is an infecting pest around the globe.

☐ Owners of properties (homes, premises) reject a reduction of rental prices; preferring to leave them empty for years.

☐ The good will never win simply because it is good; and not a lot people want to live and strengthen the good.

Psychology and Politics

☐ Politics as a core institution of society is never ready for critical self-reflection, pioneering projects, and renewal.

☐ People must be preoccupied with sorrow and fear so that leaders can operate in their own mad interests.

☐ People must be occupied with suffering in the soul so that the religion can operate in their own sick interests.

☐ People must be used to regulations, norms, all kind of accreditations, in order to be forced into obedience.

☐ The entire humanity is mentally contaminated with a history full of evil and mad doing, of lies, falseness, fabrications, and wars.

☐ It is rarely possible to pursue a career with integrity, ability to love, the truth, and with good spiritual attitudes.

☐ Contamination, poverty, and mega-cities are designed to degenerate, dehumanize, and mentally weaken the masses.

☐ All kind of catastrophes are good because it strongly limits people's life and success, happiness, participation.

☐ Public education as a core educational institution is never ready for critical self-reflection and renewal.

Psychology and Businesses

☐ The cadre of economics and the big Western corporate groups are never ready for critical self-reflection and renewal.

☐ The media corporate groups would never inform humanity about urgent indispensable renewal, nor do they accept any educational responsibility.

☐ The big media will never give up their concepts of deceit, distortion, manipulation, and brainwashing (etc.).

☐ The media abuse freedom of speech; are used to shape collective attitudes, to discredit individuals, institutions, and entire states.

☐ No super-pioneer, prophet, or Messiah (Mahdi) will ever have the media power to reach humanity.

☐ Speculations in most big businesses: Investors are never ready to abdicate speculation profit or any 'casino-games'.

☐ Interests of loans and mortgages: Investors are never ready to abdicate highest possible profit; the entire interest-concept is a pure money multiplier.

☐ Most owners of businesses are unable to deal with pioneering ideas, visions and reject any new sustainable concept.

Psychology and Religion

☐ Religion as a core educational institution is never ready for critical self-reflection and renewal; they have lost the Archetypes of the Soul.

☐ Organized religion (The Church) has much more hidden power than most people could imagine, and renewal is not possible.

☐ The falsified, distorted, and mad religions, with sources in Abraham (Moses), reject any new prophet or Messiah.

☐ Most followers of a religion are addicted to a religious psychosis and will never give up dogmatic and fundamentalist belief.

Psychology and Leadership

☐ The world is predominantly in the hands of psychopaths, megalomaniacs: renewal is not possible.

☐ The super-elite driven by a pseudo-religious mission and by psychosis are never ready for critical self-reflection and renewal.

☐ The Western world, economics, and politics are in the money grip of 6 families through their banking power: renewal is not possible.

☐ Politicians, economists, and leaders in other institutions of society have no time for personal further education.

☐ Constructive communication with psychopaths, megalomaniacs, psychotic or false and neurotic people is not possible.

☐ Politicians do not want to risk their career with pioneering projects and a new understanding of human life and society.

☐ Those who rule the world will never want an advanced democratic republic with informed and educated people.

☐ The state of humanity is purposefully created by the ultra-high net worth individuals (UHNWIs) to rule the world.

☐ Those who dispose of 80% of the global wealth will never accept a balanced distribution of money and wealth.

Psychology and Unemployment

☐ In many countries the rate of unemployment is disastrous: 8-25% and up to 30-50% of the youth do not have a job.

☐ Hundreds of millions worldwide do not have a job! Billions of people are underemployed or get a wage that does not allow for a humane life.

☐ 80% of working people in the industrial nations fear losing their job and see no good future perspectives.

☐ Many well-educated professionals are finding it difficult if not impossible to find a decent and suitable job or they are simply underpaid.

☐ For more and more couples, the creation of a family becomes a financial nightmare; love is gone and the relationship a permanent stress.

☐ Additionally, real estate, food, and consumer goods are all becoming more expensive; but the wages have stagnated or decreased since a decade.

The Essence for Psychology

The behavior of human beings is essentially a result of the way their mental functions are shaped. The science of Psychology ignores most important mental functions (e.g. the psychical energy, the spiritual intelligence).

It seems today that society's environment destroys any effort for a constructive education of the psychical functions.

Humans can't properly make their living and develop evolutionary without well-formed psychical functions of the 'I', the control and management center that every human has.

Humans also need to form and use all the cognitive functions for a successful living and development: perception, attentiveness, language, thinking, interpretation, judging, etc.

Emotions (feelings) are of enormous richness. They all have their own meaning. They are indispensable for human life.

But by letting a world full of emotions act without understanding and beyond control, they destroy human life and hinder the constructive living.

Humans produce psychical energy with their thinking, emotions, and their unconscious complexes. They infect others and the environment with their formed energy. Above that it can make one physically and mentally ill.

The science of Psychology contributes to failure in the life of billions of humans and with that especially to the archaic-regressive evolution of the collective.

1. Behavior – Actions

Essential theses

The human shapes the world, his relationships and gives way to the formation of his psychical functions.

Our daily actions are determined by our psychical functions.

The action is always in a life system and is also influenced by this.

Human life carries many risks and opportunities.

In every action is a goal and thus also a value.

Every action influences us, others, and the areas of life around us.

Many actions have 'critical' aspects, such as, wrong or no effects, side effects, are inappropriate for the situation, of an insecure state, poorly controlled or difficult to control, with external influences, and so on.

Much damage, suffering and misfortune are created by humans wrong and improperly shaped mental functions.

1.1. Actions in the Habitat

1.1.1. The human in the habitat

All our actions are controlled by psychical functions if we refrain from physiological forces. Our life consists of actions. We trade all day, from awakening to falling asleep. All human actions happen in a 'living space'.

We can subdivide this living space into systems, for example: home, workplace, relationships, school, environment, and so on. With our actions we influence the systems of the living space. We design them, influence them, and develop them. We draw from them and use them. Sometimes people damage and destroy these systems of life.

Conversely, these systems also form the psychical life. They limit the scope for action. A human is bound to his life systems and can only live through them and in them.

Everything that we perceive, think, feel, fantasize, dream, wish, and do, takes place within the various systems of life. Thus, there is an interaction between the psychic organism and the habitat.

The psychical functions are also the 'bridge' to other people. Without mental life, no human relationship is conceivable. To do this, people can use all their powers or refrain from intelligence, spirit, and love.

What the 'News' shows us daily, what newspapers and magazines tell us, and what is written in books about mankind and what a human does informs us about the work of the psychical functions. Humans always act out of the situation of their formed psychical functions.

A human being also lives in the boundaries of the habitat that people have created and continue creating. The collective psychical life of the people affects the individuals. And everyone works in his own way on the collective psychical aspects of life.

So, all people are in a complicated network that our ancestors have created and that we continue to develop daily. On a small scale, we have created happiness and unhappiness, joy and grief, problems and conflicts, hardship, and suffering. As part of the human community, we contribute to "big problems" and to great harm and suffering, such as, environmental destruction, violence, and war.

Thus, history is the result of the formed psychical functions: the past forms the present and the present determines the future. This applies to the psychical inner world and the individual life as well as to the outside world and the collective life.

The external life and the lifestyle of the people are an expression of the preceding human education. If we want to understand the external life, we must turn to the psychical life and its formation (shaping) process.

Reflections and Discussion

We are all born into a habitat. Being human and living without a living space is unthinkable. The psychical system can only develop and express itself in a habitat. Mankind is shaped by this habitat; and mankind forms the habitat. This space is an expression of the formed psychical functions.

Habitat includes:

☐ Parents, family, siblings
☐ Living area
☐ Surrounding area
☐ Goods, furniture, car
☐ Built environment
☐ Institutions
☐ Economy / Industry
☐ Other people
☐ Work
☐ Education
☐ Holiday and leisure areas
☐ Food
☐ Institutions of religion, ethics
☐ Nature and wildlife

Just as the psychical life is a complex system, so the habitat is a complex system of life.

Human action interacts with psyche-habitat (mental functions-habitat).

Important mutual aspects are:

- ☐ The life systems affect humans
- ☐ Man designs the life system.
- ☐ Man uses life systems for his life
- ☐ The life systems limit people in their actions
- ☐ The life systems are necessary
- ☐ Man can destroy life systems
- ☐ Life systems (or elements of them) can harm people.
- ☐ Each person creates his space in these life systems.

From birth to death, man is bound in the habitat and yet has a certain amount of free space in his life. In this there are risks and opportunities for humans.

Diagram 1.1.1: The human and his habitat

Diagramm OS2-1: Der Mensch und seine Lebenssysteme

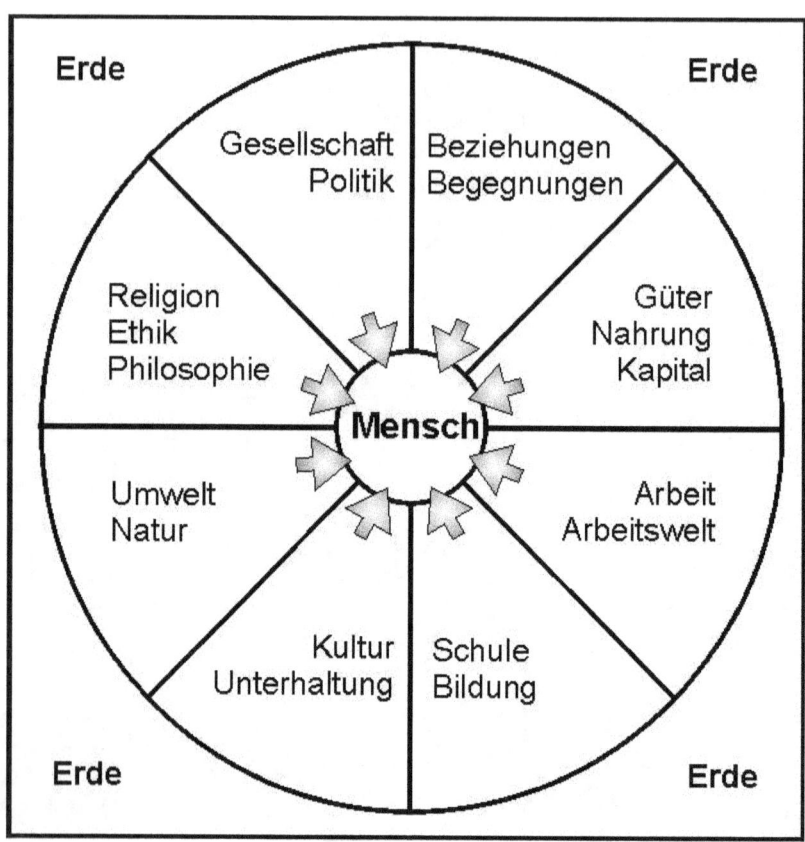

English Translation: On **earth humans** are influenced by society & politics / relations & meetings / religion, ethics & philosophy / goods, food & capital / environment & nature / job & working world / culture & entertainment / school & formation

'Actions' in theoretical reflection

An action is considered a repetition if two action situations have the same structure. Example: preparing breakfast, cleaning up the living room, buying clothes, watching TV, driving, sex in marriage (after years in everyday life). Such actions are usually considered an expression of a habit.

Action schemes are repeatable, transferable to new tasks and to new situations. Example: Discussion of a dispute with the life partner or with a friend in a recreational situation, occupational situation: doing correspondence or selling something, teaching about the same substance with different groups (students). The Acting is a system of over- and subordination of larger and smaller units associated with each other, the action steps are in chronological order, i.e. "a path from a starting point to an end point". Example: Plan sales pitch or monthly budget with the life partner.

The subjective experience of an action is the consciousness of purpose, planning, control, and intention. The core problem, however, is that humans often have vague goals in mind. As a result, little planning goes into the steps that are needed to be taken and thus leads to spontaneously moving forward, resulting in one's own actions being seldomly checked, and whether their actions are appropriate and have led them to their desired success. Side effects often occur that were neither intended nor expected; in addition, unexpected influences (facts, events, incidents) change the purpose and course.

The core aspects of the theory of actions are:

☐ The action includes a frame.
☐ Action is an inter-relationship of elements to achieve a goal.
☐ Goals are results that lie in the future.
☐ Planning requires goals.
☐ Plans and strategies guide the execution of actions.
☐ People act purposefully; often aimless and unconscious.
☐ Action is a central psychological category.
☐ Needs, decisions, awareness, will and love.
☐ The life biography determines the pattern of the actions.
☐ Action is future-oriented, intentional, purposeful, potentially and fully aware.
☐ Actions include: Course, level of complexity, and situation.
☐ To the course: Beginning, course and final phase.
☐ Action phases include: Affective, structural and energetic aspects.
☐ Meaning of actions are set arbitrarily.

☐ It is possible to determine the outcome of the action's.

☐ Actions can be assessed and the subject blamed.

☐ Situation elements receive their psychological significance in the course of action.

☐ The assessment of the achievement of the goal creates a sense of 'Self'.

☐ Culture is the reification of actions.

Practical learning about daily action

The different teaching and learning methods of adult education enable the topic 'action' and others following practical approaches:

Two partners interview each other on the basis of a few questions:

☐ What are your favorite actions in your day to day life?

☐ Which action situations are you most excited about?

☐ How is your sense of 'Self' at a glance about all the effects of a day?

☐ Where do you have a lot/little action energy?

Questions are collected in a group: What do you think about questions if you want to take a closer look at your actions over a week? Examples: When? Why? As? For what? How often? Together? With who? Etc.

Create a list of 10 typical everyday actions. Then try to formulate an alternative to each action.

Name an important life goal for yourself! Which daily actions are "partial actions" regarding this goal achievement? And what actions hinder or block this achievement?

Formulate new ideas for some everyday action areas. Then, what changes can arise in your life if you translate these ideas into concrete action?

Role play (in a group, in the family, in the workplace). Select a problem-prone action situation from one area of life where other people are involved. Distribute the roles and play through situation and alternatives. Then discuss the most efficient options for action.

Take another action situation. Disassemble them into their elements. Then formulate theses on each element according to the pattern:

a) the bigger ... the smaller
b) the smaller ... the bigger
c) the less ... the more
d) the more ... the less
e) the stronger ... the stronger
f) the weaker ... the weaker
g) the less ... the less
h) the more ... the more

Group work: In a group, collect potential constructive (beneficial) remedies for a particular type of action (e.g. talk with the partner, shopping, driving, personal care, cooking).

Group work: Collect some actions into a typical everyday situation that calls for an action. Then create a "Mind-Mapping" for the "type of action": in the center, the keyword, then many main and secondary lines, which show the networks.

Take some typical everyday actions again. Then, formulate the responsibility of the acting person as well as the limits of responsibility.

Give to a 'difficult' action a new framework: exchange elements with others. Change the order of the steps. Try to imagine the opposite. Change the destination.

Notes and Perspectives

What is the purpose of reflecting on one's own actions in everyday life?

Write down the key words in this subchapter:

What function do life systems have for humans?

Reflecting on the relationship between human and life systems is essential because:

What did you learn about the function of life systems in your parents' home, school, and church?

What significance in living together has the conversation about actions?

How is networked action in politics and the economy shown?

What does advertising convey about people's actions?

Formulate an important question about networked actions.

1.1.2. Life risks and life chances

Conflicts, difficulties, problems, and life-suffering belong in everyone's life. Such challenges are inevitable. Man is constantly exposed to new situations throughout his life.

There is no relationship between two people without problems. Mother and father roles are shaped by the developmental growth of the children.

Career advancement or changes, including the years of continuity of a work situation, lead to mental reactions. In addition, worrying about money, holidays and leisure time, birth, and death in one's own network of relationships as well as much more affect physical activity.

Stress, aggression, inner emptiness, loneliness, fears and hopes and much more combined with feelings, thoughts, needs, desires are expressions of the vivid inner life and all also leave their mark.

Violence, accidents of all kinds, addictions, suicides and attempted suicide, guilt and crime always have something to do with the psychical life.

Psychical forces cause much harm, unhappiness and suffering in society. For example, through: Wrong perception and thinking, thoughtlessness, unprocessed feelings, lack of concentration, wrong self-assessment, bad communication, unadopted behavior, missing foresight, indifference, unrealistic ideals, wrong attitudes, missing love, no conscious cultivation of meaning and no one's own duty towards human values, etc.

Apparently, the psychical functions 'make' our lives.

Stressful effects also result from the psychical forces in the life systems.

We pollute the environment, destroy the habitat, exploit resources, produce waste problems, and build an alienating environment. We produce goods that do not have the least value. We create natural disasters through obstruction.

Many are not able to control the many influences from the life systems; overburdened by suppression and repression.

We are facing enormous problems in the international, political, and economic sphere, such as: Poverty, migration, unemployment, hunger, riots, and wars.

Here, too, psychical forces of the people are always at work. Political mistakes, power politics, greed, ideologies, and religious attitudes are forces from the mental life. Ideal systems and religious teachings are related to psychical life.

What sects and psycho-religious movements teach and do comes from the inner life, the disfigured unconscious, and the way their mental functions are shaped.

Thoughts, feelings, needs, and fantasies are formed into 'theories' or 'propositions'. Values and norms are derived from this. After that man should live and the national life be shaped.

Where this always leads, history shows us.

Reflections and Discussion

Obviously, life in the systemic interconnectedness called "mental system and living space", is risky:

- ☐ Related to ourselves (physically, psychically).
- ☐ Related to others (physically, psychically, socially).
- ☐ Related to the habitat (nature and wildlife).
- ☐ Related to the social and social life.

The personal psychical risks include:

- ☐ Stress, restlessness
- ☐ Inner emptiness, meaninglessness
- ☐ Hopelessness
- ☐ Fears
- ☐ Desperation
- ☐ Fainting
- ☐ Loneliness
- ☐ Related disorders
- ☐ Displeasure
- ☐ Lack of love

We all stand in a life course with different phases, and thus with different, phase-specific risks:

School - apprenticeship - marriage - children - the "so-called 7th year" - increasing professional responsibility (career) - increasing need for money - various different life disappointments - midlife crisis - the inner life termination often before the age of 50 years - retirement - old age, often with illness and suffering.

Our fathers and mothers have taken over the habitat and shaped it further. They shaped us too.

We take over this world and continue to shape it. We shape our children and our risks.

Therefore: the past forms the psyche and determines the present; the present is again the past of the future. Our life risks are in this network.

In this system integration and historicity, we have our chances for self-education and self-realization:

☐ Luck	☐ Hope	☐ Peace
☐ Joy	☐ Meaning of life	☐ Fulfillment

Diagram 1.1.2: The central life risks

Diagramm OS2-2: Die zentralen Lebensrisiken

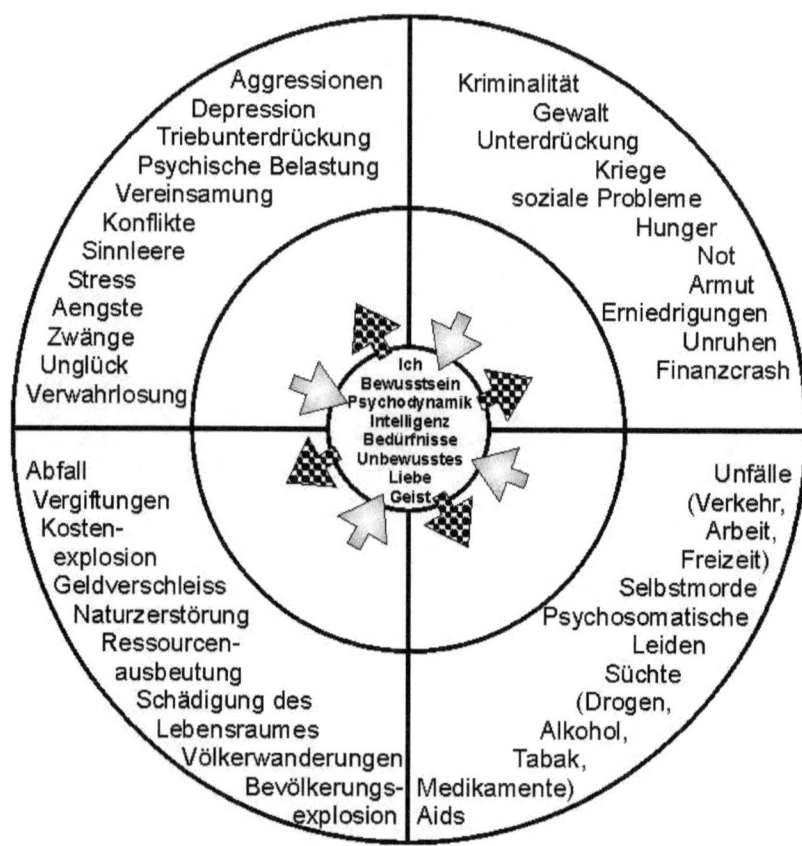

English Translation: Aggression, depression, suppression of drive, psychical pressure, isolation, conflicts, lack of sense, stress, fears, bondages, disaster, neglect / Criminality, violence, suppression, wars, social problems, hunger, misery, poverty, humiliation, riots, financial crash / Waste, intoxications, explosion of costs, waste of money, damage of nature, exploitation of resources, damage of environment, migrations, explosion of population / Accidents (Traffic, work, leisure), suicides, psycho-somatic suffering, addictions (Drogues, alcohol, tobacco, medicines), Aids interact with **the "I", conscious, psycho-dynamic, intelligence, needs, unconscious, love, spirit.**

Action capacities in the life course (CV)

Action capacities in the curriculum vitae are of outstanding importance in the context of basic life risks and life chances. Because, in a positive way, this means:

The competences achieved in a development phase can be understood as prerequisites and consequences for the following development steps. If the coordination and organization of personal resources succeeds in a phase of life, then a good mastering of future challenges is to be expected.

A competent individual can use the environmental resources and the personal resources in such a way that a good outcome for the personal development is given.

Social and technological change, as well as psychical and physical changes, requiring the constant adaptation of the behavioral repertoire to the associated processing and coping capacities in order to create and coordinate flexible, adequate responses to environmental demands, and the opportunities for action that our social environment offers to exploit.

Short and simple: Competent skills are needed to cope with real needs: these are formed from early childhood.

The biographical retrospective makes it possible for self-reflection and to record development-related capacities or weak points. According to the guidelines for vulnerabilities (that primarily affect the personal life), the greater the vulnerabilities, the higher the risks to life and vice versa.

During early childhood: The building of basic trust, social attachment, symbolic and linguistic expressiveness.

During late childhood: Coping with contemporaries, appropriate male and female role behaviors, concepts and thinking patterns (necessary for everyday life), building conscience, positive attitude to oneself as a growing organism.

During early adolescence: School performance, relations with peers of both sexes, assumption of male and female gender roles, acceptance of one's own physical appearance, body management.

<u>During late adolescence:</u> Abstract intellectual operations, emotional independence of parents and other adults, preparation for marriage and family life, system value as a guide to behavior, stable self-image and self-identity, use of the consumer goods market.

<u>During early adulthood:</u> Selecting a partner, building a partner relationship, starting a family, reflexive person-environment relationships in the social context, organizing the household, taking responsibility as a citizen, finding a lifestyle.

<u>During late adulthood:</u> Detachment from one's own children, consolidation, and constant redefinition of the partner relationship, directing energies to new roles and tasks, accepting one's own lived life.

In every stage of life, a mismatch between social, psychical, and physical demands on the one hand and one's own capacity for action on the other hand can occur and be experienced as threatening or stressful. In addition, weak points significantly increase the personal life risks.

Conclusion: Life risks and life chances can be regulated by the subject of the action within certain limits and are dependent on the personal development of psychologically formed resources.

Biographical vulnerabilities from action and competences

Mark those that apply:

☐ No vulnerability   ☐ Vulnerability   ☻ High vulnerability

☐ Prenatal rejection
☐ Rigid, irregular and rather cold care in infancy
☐ Emotionally burdened parent relationship (atmosphere) in early childhood
☐ Rather little emotional attention and thus parent-attachment disorders
☐ Rigid cleanliness and order education
☐ Strict, rigid parenting behavior
☐ Difficult and negative sibling relations
☐ Burdens in the social system of leisure and school (comrades, friends)
☐ Lack of education and enlightenment
☐ Strong dogmatic and mythological religious education
☐ Overemphasis on intellectual abilities
☐ Little scope for creativity
☐ Consumer-oriented leisure time (television, etc.)
☐ Parents with financial difficulties
☐ Many quarrels between parents, with little constructive communication
☐ Disturbed relationships with mother, father, siblings, teachers, pastors
☐ Diseases and accidents (own and those of parents and siblings)
☐ Move and change of school
☐ Divorce of parents, remarriage (stepmother / -father)
☐ No clear structures and standards in the household
☐ Addictive behavior of parents (alcohol, tobacco, drugs, sweets, etc.)
☐ Little emotional support from relatives, neighbors, family acquaintances
☐ A stressful first sexual experience
☐ Failed early friendships
☐ Poor possibilities of counseling and support from teacher, pastor
☐ Unemployment of the father
☐ Dissatisfaction of the mother, e.g. due to missing / unsatisfactory work
☐ A lot of parental defense in conflict resolution and communication
☐ School failures and corresponding discrimination
☐ Own unemployment after school, vocational training
☐ Unhappiness/ failure in building one's life (young adulthood)
☐ Increased mental susceptibility even in childhood and adolescence
☐ Little support in building trust in one's own ability
☐ Strong inferiority feelings over years of childhood and adolescence
☐ Separation (for example, death, departure) of loved ones
☐ Deficits in basic needs (love, recognition, community, etc.)
☐ Little consideration of one's inner life (feelings, thinking, etc.)

- [ ] Rigid power behavior of people in the living environment
- [ ] Violence and warlike events in the extended living environment
- [ ] Little conscious development of one's own action-oriented standards
- [ ] Little life knowledge of the parents and those in one's close environment
- [ ] Suppression and general defense against "problems"
- [ ] Little opportunity to acquire knowledge about the psychic life
- [ ] Little love experiences, but a lot of "fight" experiences
- [ ] Much hatred, envy, greed, aggression, jealousy, frustration, living, etc.
- [ ] Tendency of dishonesty in the living environment (life lies)
- [ ] Little room for personal engagement
- [ ] Little acceptance of imagination, dreams, and inner picture viewing
- [ ] Tendency to have an overload of requirements and services (stress)
- [ ] Little experience of reconciliation in the many everyday concerns
- [ ] Rigid thinking patterns in the home, at school and workplace
- [ ] Learned images of God, ideas about the hereafter without inner experience
- [ ] No systematic handling of one's own lived biography (processing)

Notes and Perspectives

What is the use of thinking about life risks?

Write down the key words in this subchapter:

What impact do the life risks have on everyday life?

Reflecting on biographical vulnerabilities is essential because: ...

What did you learn about biographical "weak spots" in your parents' home, school, and church?

What significance, when living together, does the discussion about life risks have?

How are life risks reduced by politics and the economy?

What does advertising convey about life risks?

Formulate an important question about the collective significance of individual risky actions:

1.1.3. Critical actions

Our actions become 'critical' if we do not know how to act; or have trouble acting right; or by acting to create a 'problem' for us and/or others.

Such "critical actions" are for example:

Talking to a partner about a difficulty, creating free time, looking for a partner for a relationship and/or sex, planning vacations, housing, buying consumer goods, taking out insurance, looking for a job, starting a career, raising children, regulating TV consumption, cleaning, washing clothes and cooking, and much more.

Every day we can see, if we look closely, that some actions are 'critical' in the sense mentioned above.

There is a lack of skills. We do not know how to decide. We do not consider the goal of an action. Or we do something that we did not intend to do that way.

Sometimes we do not grasp what has moved a particular action in us. Internal psychical forces and/or external factors determine how we behave in all possible situations.

Every person seeks happiness and meaning in his own way. Much of what we do is focused on experiencing joy and pleasure, finding contentment, or living with deeper values.

As part of the course of one's life, human beings also focus on specific topics: relationship, children, job, leisure, and age. Even goods and entertainment should contribute to happiness.

- ☐ How do people consider their happiness when they are asked?
- ☐ How do you deal with your inner life as a condition of possibilities?
- ☐ How do you react to your inner life that interferes with desired happiness?
- ☐ How do you anticipate the goal of the plot?
- ☐ How do you deal with patterns of action that always lead to failure?
- ☐ People also search for happiness under a religious dimension.
- ☐ What are their inner sources for the foundation of belief?

Acting means 'living'. There is a lot to do for everyone: to shape the autonomous life with relations and work, to give home and leisure its own style, to realize professional plans, to fulfill obligations for the state and to manage life administration.

Where and how do people learn to act properly and effectively in all life issues?

What should be done if action is experienced as 'critical'?

Reflections and Discussion

We always act with our psychical forces, regardless of whether we consciously grasp and deliberately control it or not.

The action can be considered under the following aspects:

☐ The habitat in which the action happens
☐ The action itself
☐ The goal or effect of the action
☐ The psychic forces involved in it

Many actions are 'critical', that is:

☐ The action contains a problem that requires a decision
☐ There is an operational difficulty due to lack of skills
☐ The effects are different to what is expected
☐ There are unexpected and unwanted side effects
☐ The goals are not reached with the chosen actions
☐ The habitat offers action limits
☐ The psychical life has a limiting or disturbing effect on the action

In every action we can also recognize a value. This value can be related to the intention, or even be experienced independently:

useful	useless	great	liberating
damaging	harmful	evil	burdening
constructively	stupid	satisfactory	embarrassing

Main questions are focused on the habitat:

☐ How do individual life systems influence the action?
☐ Which people take influence of the actions?

☐ Which determinant limits the scope of action or triggers a certain action?
☐ What influence do people and elements of life systems have on 'successful' action?

The other main questions are directed to the psychic organism:

☐ How do the individual psychical subsystems and forces affect action?
☐ How do you disrupt the action?
☐ How do you push for action?
☐ What influence do you have on 'successful' actions?

Diagram 1.1.3: The main components of actions

Diagramm OS2-3: Die Hauptkomponenten von Handlungen

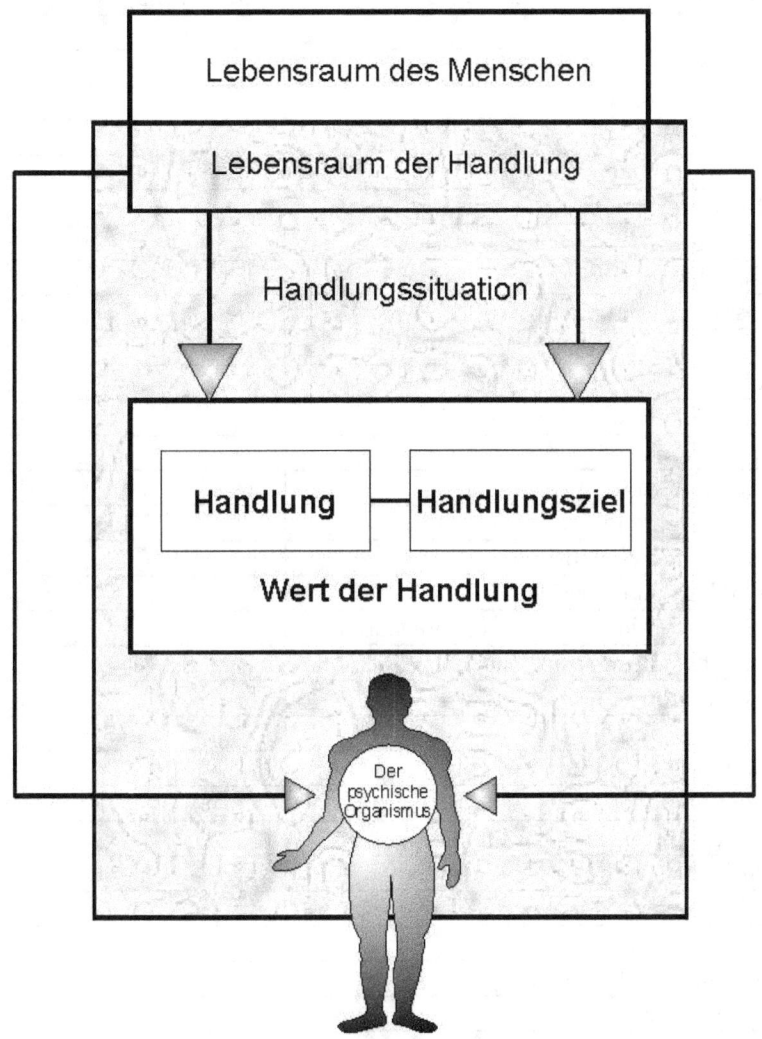

English Translation: Habitat of humans, habitat of actions, situation of action, action, aim of action, value of action effect the psychical organism.

Skills competences to critical situations

Write down your assumptions and ideas about how to react/to solve:

Critical action, critical situation:	Skills to manage it:
Stress	
Quarrel with your life partner	
Need of money	
Birth of one's own child	
Unemployment	
Divorce	
Moving	
Changing jobs	
Loss of a loved one (death)	
Inclusion of own children	
Sexual desire and no partner	
Alone and desire for a partner	
Promotion	
Excessive food	
Alone during the holidays	
'Immature' relationship	
Boredom on the weekend	
Loss of confidence in the relationship	
Out of wedlock sexual experience	
Distribution of household work	
Intense dream life	
Inhibitions in communication	
Inner emptiness	
Aggression against your life partner	
Difficulties with your own children	
Debt and payment shortage	
Unable to express feelings	
Too much TV consumption	
Dull sex life	
Overwork at the workplace	
Poor quality of living (noise, exhaust gases)	
General experience of futility	
Feelings of inferiority	

Un-lust, lethargic boredom, dissatisfaction	
Beginning retirement	
Slight flu susceptibility	
Humiliations from others	
Quarrel with father-in-law/mother	
Allegations from the mother about lifestyle	
Dispute with partner over TV program selection	
Disorder in the home	
Controversy over religious dogmas in the family	
Political differences with the father	
Unjustified criticism from a friend	
Quarrel about weekend plans with your partner	
Bad body feeling	
Allegations from the supervisor/employer	

Critical life events during the course of life

There are different events for each person over the course of their life, like certain actions. Some can be referred to as 'critical'. This may not be the actual action, but the event in the center of the situation.

Elementary characteristics of such life events are:

The central definition of "critical events" is stressful, i.e., objectively describable situations where confrontation is generally stressful and involves an experience that either imposes grief or requires a role transformation.

Characteristics of critical life events include personal disaster (severe illness), age-related occurrence (puberty), historical facts (wars), natural events (disasters), central CV characteristics (e.g., marriage) and unique non-normative events (divorce, death).

Critical life events include: early days, puberty, first menstruation, marriage, childbirth, illness, divorce, death of a loved one, career advancement/descent, menopause, retirement, wars, technological change, economic crises, migration, stress, victims (perpetrator) of a criminal act, promotion, inheritance, a move, unemployment, school career end, leaving of the last child from the parental home, widowhood, retirement home, and so on.

Strategies to cope with "critical events" are:

☐ Positive reinterpretation	☐ Hope/optimism
☐ Perception defense	☐ Explicit affirmation of a situation
☐ Simplify	☐ Fatalism
☐ Rationalize	☐ Taking up help and opportunities
☐ Displacing	☐ Distraction
☐ Projecting	☐ Shift to substitute actions
☐ Somatic reaction formation	☐ Self-influence (suggestion)
☐ Delayed action	☐ Going out of the field (escape)
☐ Active action	☐ Anxiety reaction, depression
☐ Personal commitment	☐ Expressing anger/grief
☐ Confidence in your own ability	☐ Restructuring the value scale
☐ Information search	☐ Understanding the limits of one's own ability
☐ Self-reflection	
☐ Adaptation to the situation	☐ Correction of own expectations
☐ Alignment to authorities	

No constructive management is possible with:

☐ Superficial perception
☐ Making fun of
☐ Being negative
☐ Being cynical
☐ Assigning own guilt to others
☐ Analyzing inaccurately
☐ Being indifferent
☐ Leaving the solution to others
☐ Not important/serious
☐ Not wanting to understand
☐ Not wanting to learn anything new
☐ Only defying and scolding
☐ Being overbearing about 'problems'

Notes and Perspectives

What is the purpose of editing critical action situations?

Write down the key words in this subchapter:

What happens in the long term to those people who have not learned any skills to cope?

Reflecting on critical life events is essential because: ...

What did you learn in the home, school, and church about managing critical life situations?

What meaning, when living together, has the conversation about critical actions and critical events taught you?

How is the reaction of individual people in politics and business considered?

What does advertising convey about critical events?

Formulate an important question about coping skills:

1.1.4. Exercises

1. Which habitat components particularly influenced you?

2. How do you influence your living space through your daily life?

3. What are your daily "critical actions"? (Give 3 examples.)

4. What is particularly typical of your "critical actions" in the monthly review?

5. Which of your psychical functions cause 'critical' actions?

6. What external factors create 'critical' situations?

7. Where does it lead if you never change (improve) your typical behavior?

8. What do you want to improve (redesign) in your daily activities?

9. Circle where you experience your own "critical life situations":

- Dining
- Communication with spouse
- Drinking
- Throat
- Shopping
- Holiday season, how to spend holidays
- Watching TV
- Handling waste
- Making a call
- Driving a car
- Household work
- Products (for purchase)
- Selling something
- How you spend free time
- Sex
- Playing
- Education
- Seeking relationship or partner
- Practicing religion
- Disorder in the home
- Evening activities
- Weekend (how it is spent)
- Restricting others, hindering them
- Cheating
- Sadistic torture
- Being violent
- Handling money
- Causing accidents
- Design of living/home decor
- Getting sick
- Drug consumption
- Punishing others
- Dealing with others (mentally)
- Allegations from your life partner
- Management of daily routines

- Negotiating situations
- Selfless actions
- Quarrelling
- Doing office work at home
- Praising someone

- Spending the evening in a bar
- Talking with acquaintances
- Celebrations
- Attending a party
- Speculating
- Reading magazines
- Sunbathing for days
- Listening to music
- Broken relationships
- Working situations of all kinds
- Anxiety behavior
- Reactions to grief
- Behavior in solitude
- Self-handling at home
- Stealing, ripping off
- Dealing with the inner life
- Dispute over religious teachings
- Internal termination (work)
- Loss of confidence
- Humiliating others
- Meaningless actions
- Professional frustrations
- Poor quality of living
- Unemployment
- Bad body sensation
- Allegations in the workplace
- Not completing 'homework'.
- Stress levels

How do you experience the overall picture of your information?

Analytical short report. My "critical event situations" – Nr...

'Critical' means insecure, uncomfortable, sensitive, conflicting, tense, embarrassing, weak, disturbing, stressful, painful, unsuccessful, in need of change, incapable of decision. Take an example from everyday life; edit this as follows:

1. The event situation: what has happened? What happened?

2. Actual act(s) in the event situation: What did you do? Who did what?

3. Life system/systems around: How was the environment? What else has influenced the event?

4. In what sense do you experience which aspects as 'critical'?

5. Prospective: What are your wishes/change of goal?

Where is the solution/solutions?

Multiple Choice Test

Select the four correct answers:

1.1. The human in the habitat. Central life systems of humans are:

- ☐ a) Relationships
- ☐ b) Work
- ☐ c) Car
- ☐ d) School/education
- ☐ e) Dream reality
- ☐ f) Environmental nature

1.2. The life risks and life chances. Central life risks are:

- ☐ a) Accidents
- ☐ b) Lack of success
- ☐ c) Inner meaninglessness
- ☐ d) Low reputation
- ☐ e) Unrelatedness
- ☐ f) Life without spirit

1.3. The actions in the habitat. Proper statements about actions are:

- ☐ a) Critical actions are only those criticized by others.
- ☐ b) Actions are independent of meaning and value questions.
- ☐ c) Actions are always an expression of psychic powers.
- ☐ d) Acts always happen in life systems.
- ☐ e) Man can act unconsciously.
- ☐ f) Actions are in the field of tension "mental system of life".

1.2. Systemic Interdependencies of Actions

1.2.1. The elements of actions

Life always means action. The dormant man is in dormant action. So, we can say that also doing nothing and sleeping are "actions". Almost all actions are the result of learning processes. We can only act the way we have learned.

In known situations we repeat the learned patterns. In new situations, we draw on the obvious possibilities from the existing repertoire.

If we change one way to act, or learn a new course of action, then a new situation has been developed. This becomes a new action. Without learning new actions, conflicts can arise. This can be through a collision or through lack of success.

Nobody should want to say that they do not have a new behavior (action) to learn.

We can change an action by first analyzing it and then by breaking it down into smaller components. The core elements known are: the actual action, the goal (the effect) and the value that lies within. In addition, we can examine the action in the context of the situation and grasp the connections with the psychic system.

The first extension is the retrospective: how did this pattern of action come about? What is the history of learning and experiencing this specific action? This is the "retrospective".

On the other hand, we can also look to the future: where does this lead if this way of acting always remains the same in such situations? And, what is the desirable development?

Of course, we cannot investigate a thousand different actions. It is enough for us to work on the so-called "critical action situations" more precisely. Hardly anyone will never experience such 'critical' moments. Some people regularly experience such action situations daily, others perhaps weekly.

A first general overview helps us to recognize the need for learning.

Reflections and Discussion

Analyzing and re-learning is based on:

Every action is a manifestation of a certain quality.
Every action has one goal or one effect (the result).
Every action contains a value for the agent.
Each story contains a history of learning and experience.
An action includes the future through anticipation and repetition.
An action cannot be adequately described without the situation.
Every action affects the person and components of the situation.
An action is always an 'event', of short or longer duration.

Theoretical rewrites to "critical event situation". 'Critical' means one or more of the following elements:

☐ Change
☐ Dependence
☐ Novel experience
☐ Collision
☐ Choice Variation
☐ Control problem
☐ Stagnation

☐ Unwanted effect
☐ Sense question
☐ Decision problem
☐ Aimlessness
☐ Execution problem
☐ Reflecting interest

An approach allows the following checklist, which can be weighted with "this applies to me ...":

☐ My actions do not affect what I want to achieve with them.
☐ I wish that my actions will do better in the future.
☐ My actions lead to stressful situations.
☐ I do not know for what purpose I act the way I do.
☐ I act without knowing exactly why I am doing so.
☐ I act without knowing what pushes me from within.
☐ I wish to understand my actions better.
☐ I experience uncertainty in my actions.
☐ I keep acting the same way as before.
☐ In different situations, I want to be able to act differently.
☐ I do not think much about my actions.
☐ I cannot decide how to act.
☐ My way of acting leads to conflicts again and again.
☐ I experience myself in action without motivation.

☐ I am not very conscious in the daily routine.
☐ I experience many things that I do, as meaningless and questionable.

Diagram 1.2.1: The extended model system of actions

Diagramm OS2-4: Das erweiterte Systemmodell der Handlungen

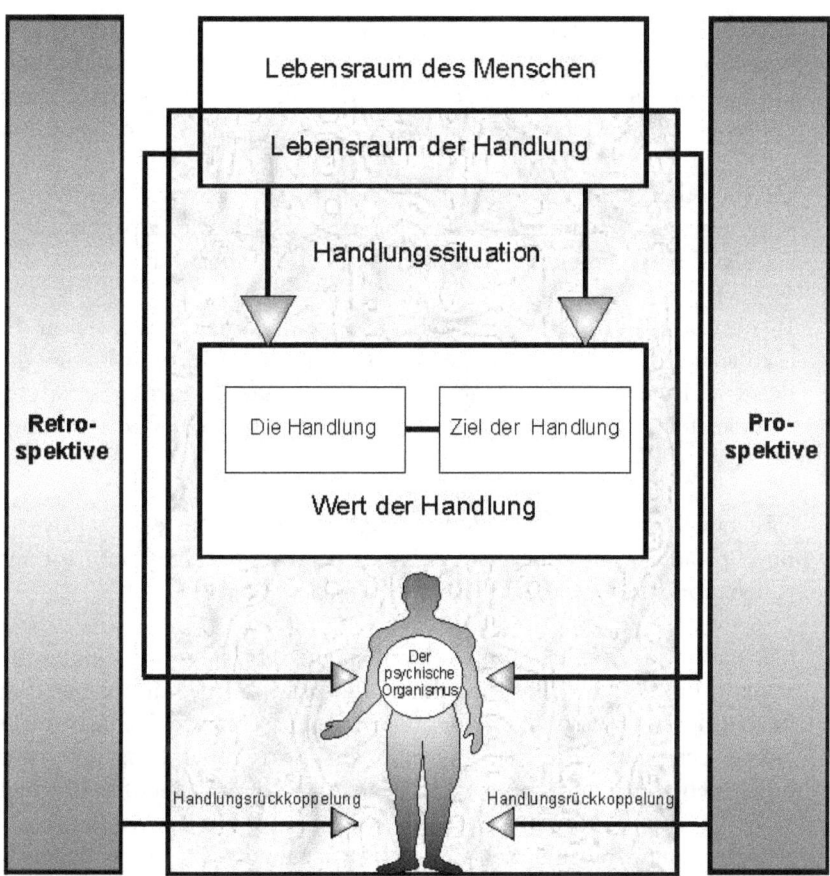

English Translation: Feedbacks from the retrospective and the prospective, habitat of humans and of actions, the situation of action, action itself, the aim of action, the value of action to the psychological organism.

1.2.2. Critical life issues

There are certain life events that are 'critical' due to their uniqueness and particularity. Others are 'critical' in that they are part of their daily activities for a lifetime. They receive their emotionally experienced value through their effect and through the experience of the action.

A change of residence can have a lasting effect on the long-term. The death of a loved one, a change of profession or the dissolution of a community of life can not only have a direct effect on daily life but can also have unexpected consequences at a later date (for example, a wrong decision or a suffering).

On the other hand, there are areas of activity that are always up to date in the same way, e.g. watching TV, driving a car, conflicts with a partner, workplace problems and much more. The effects can also be delayed.

If you watch TV for three to four hours a day for many years, repeat the same conflict patterns with your partner over many years, or maintain the well-known leisure habits again and again, you create deep-rooted patterns. The quality of the action remains unchanged. The goals or effects are always the same.

The value of such actions always reactivates the same feelings. Over time, a new "problem" or 'critical' situation arises, and life disappointment and deep resignation spread. Passivity becomes a standard pattern.

Consumption of alien life is increasingly replacing one's own life. The relationship is dead. This may make life easier on the surface but creates an increasing complexity in the depths of the psychic life. Repression leads to side effects. The oppressed is irrational. The value and meaning of life are dulled. The sense of responsibility is set to a minimal level of performance.

Experience in almost all fields of activity accumulates to the same life pattern. At the age of 50, 60 and 70, humans can no longer adequately react to their new CV situation. A human, at these ages, is preponderantly fixated in regressive action. The increased use of prejudices, ideologies and dogmatism should then justify the situation.

Reflections and Discussion

Unique "critical situations" in a life course are:

☐ Change of residence
☐ Job change
☐ Financial changes
☐ Marriage
☐ Separation
☐ Birth
☐ Disease
☐ Accident

☐ Divorce
☐ Death of a friend
☐ Unemployment
☐ Victim (crime)
☐ Transport
☐ Offense
☐ Leaving the church

Repetitive "critical actions" are:

☐ Dining
☐ Speeches
☐ Sleeping
☐ Sexuality
☐ Visits
☐ TV

☐ Going out
☐ Household chores
☐ Calls
☐ Shopping
☐ Religious practices

Effects of actions may be different in the time perspective. For example:

selectively	long term	delaying
medium term	directly/immediately	accumulating in time

The following processes are possible:

Components of action versus critical situation's quality	Quality	Target/Effect	Value Experience
e.g. Visits			
e.g. Shopping			

Diagram 1.2.2: The spectrum of "Critical life issues"

Diagramm OS2-5: Das Spektrum der "kritischen Lebensthemen"

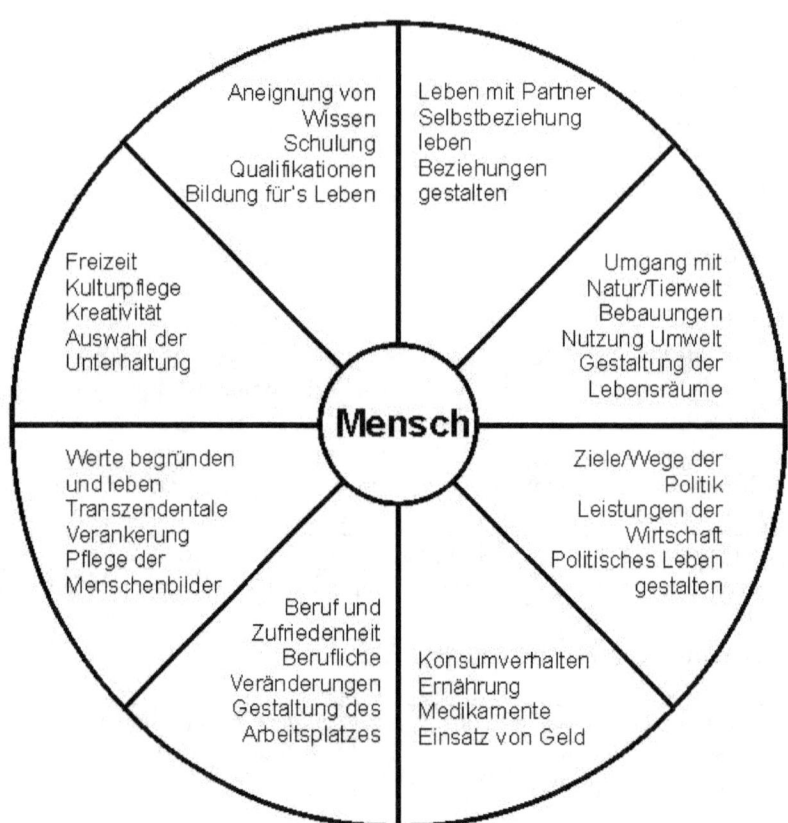

English Translation: Acquisition of knowledge, qualifications, formation for life / Live with Partner, self-relation, shaping relations / Leisure, culture, creativity, entertainment / Understanding nature, animal world, housing, using environment, habitats / Establishing values and living them, transcendental anchoring, caring of images of humans / Aims, ways of politics, benefit of economics, creating political life / Work and satisfaction, changes, creating the working place / Consumerism, alimentation, medicines, use of money

1.2.3. Habitat systems as influencing factors

Man is always multidimensionally networked with his actions. Every action can be considered in this network.

We simplify the many possibilities in three dimensions: the activities or action areas (thematic, not situation-specific), the habitats with their many systems and the reference persons (interactions).

A human being acts through his actions on these three areas. And conversely, elements from these three dimensions influence the action of the individual.

This interplay is in the time perspective, so it is constantly in motion. The same outcomes are seldom the same in the past, in the present, and in the future. They often reproduce the situation with the prehistory.

If the elements of the three dimensions change, the action becomes different. If the action always remains the same, then this should lead to tensions and action failures. 'Critical' moments result from the fact that each new situation never exactly matches the previous one.

Let us take an example: John discusses a marital conflict with Marie. The TV is running. Marie is cooking. A child is sitting in the bathtub. The neighbors have just left from the "Tea chat".

Such frameworks are unfavorable for discussion. If the neighbors were still in the room, then the action (discussion) would again be subject to other conditions. In addition, other factors are conceivable: Marie wants John to cook. John is angry because unpaid bills are on the table. Both think that they would have been better off not talking about politics with their neighbors, but about disregarding the mess in the house. John is hungry, the child is crying in the bathtub and the TV thriller has already started.

From all three dimensions, elements act in the plot. The result is unlikely to be constructive.

Reflections and Discussion

The three dimensions of action are, with examples:

1) The activities or fields of action/action topics:

☐ Work   ☐ TV   ☐ Leisure
☐ Households   ☐ Entertainment ☐ Recreation
☐ Speeches   ☐ Holiday   ☐ Mobility

2) The habitats include:

☐ Housing   ☐ Recreational places ☐ Mall
☐ Apartment of a friend   ☐ Workplace   ☐ Office
☐ Movement area   ☐ Accommodation   ☐ Institution X-Z

3) The caregivers are:

☐ Partner   ☐ Parents   ☐ Neighbors
☐ Friend   ☐ Work colleagues ☐ Related
☐ Own children   ☐ Acquaintances   ☐ Siblings

Elements from the three dimensions work through:

☐ Conduct   ☐ Lust   ☐ Stimulation
☐ Role expectation ☐ Feeling Activation ☐ Offer
☐ Character Appeal ☐ Sense Activation   ☐ Vital Necessity
☐ Obligations   ☐ Entitlement   ☐ Suggestion
☐ Need stimulation ☐ Unpretentiousness ☐ Provocations

The dimensions can be examined and reflected for each action:

Dimensions versus actions	Action area	Habitat	Caregiver
e.g. TV			
e.g. Shopping			

Diagram 1.2.3: The networking of actions

Diagramm OS2-6: Die Vernetzungen der Handlungen"

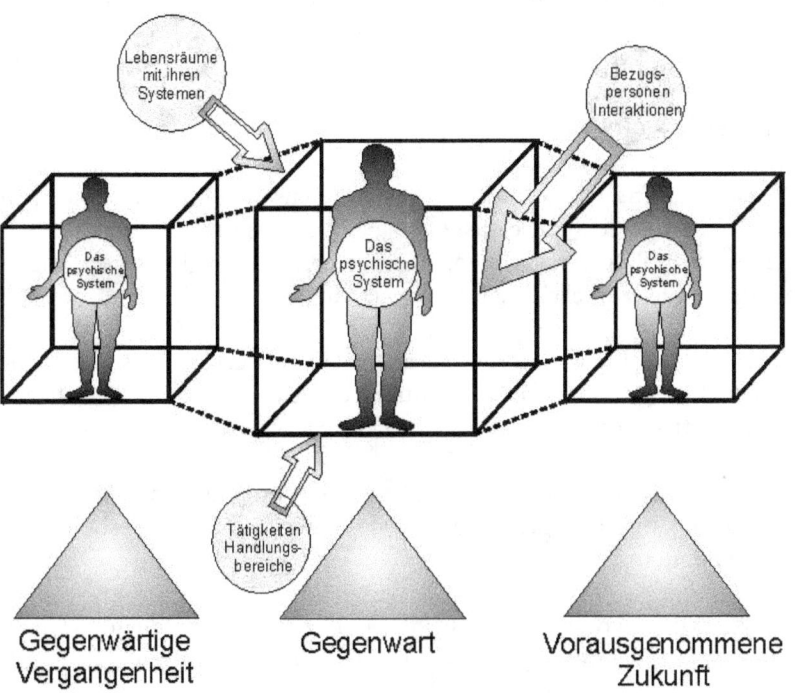

| Gegenwärtige Vergangenheit | Gegenwart | Vorausgenommene Zukunft |

English Translation: From the present past to the present and the anticipated future activities and its areas affect the psychological system as well as the systems of the habitat and the interactions with psychological parents.

1.2.4. The psychical organism as a moving force

There is no doubt that the elements of the three dimensions have a significant influence on individual actions. Eating, talking, working, watching TV and many more actions can vary daily in expression. The reasons lie partly in externally changed constellations, partly also in the psychical inner world.

The individual psychical subsystems participate in the action. Man acts differently, whether he is relaxed or tense. If his life energy is vital or weak, it has different effects.

Weak will, little self-control and much defense, with simultaneously reduced or undifferentiated consciousness, have a corresponding effect on the action. This also applies to undifferentiated perception, thoughtlessness, vague use of words and little intellectual learning activity.

The emotional state, from pleasant to unpleasant or positive to negative, "colors" the action. Likewise, unfulfilled needs and artificially activated need tension affect action.

The unconscious patterns of life (images of humans, life experiences, superego, attitudes) press humans in their actions, corresponding to the shaped patterns.

Those who work with dreams and regularly meditate with specific imaginations, let this experience affect their actions.

Thus, the power of love has a decisive influence on all action. Anyone who has built up little here is acting differently than someone who has learned to live with love and love in an all-encompassing way.

On this occasion, it should be remembered that every human being in his actions is tied back to these intrapsychic powers. This is to be considered if the caregivers are included in their influence in an action situation.

Just as humans learn how to drive a car in small learning steps, so can the actions for a particular situation be approached in the same way.

Over time, one deals with the psychical subsystems, without consciously having to deliberate and control each individual contribution - as in driving a car, where the actions become more and more automated.

Reflections and Discussion

The psychological subsystems with their sub-areas and the individual functions have a significant impact on the daily actions of every human being.

☐ The psychodynamics: Tension-relaxation, vitality and strength, etc.
☐ The "I" functions: Will, defense, integration, control, conscious content
☐ The intelligence systems: Perception, thinking, language, learning.
☐ The feelings: Life-oriented-life-averted, pleasant-unpleasant.
☐ The needs: Basic needs, artificial needs
☐ The unconscious: Life experiences, human images, superego, attitudes
☐ The spirit: Dream, imagination, contemplation
☐ Love: For oneself, for others, for nature and wildlife, for transcendence

Discuss the influences in a small group according to the following scheme. You can formulate various aspects, for example:

☐ How do emotions and food interact?
☐ What is the correlation between mind and religious practice?
☐ How does the will work when shopping?
☐ What is the interaction between sexual action and love?
☐ How does household work affect the emotions?
☐ What influence does exercise have on psychodynamics?
☐ How does the unconscious affect relationships?
☐ What is the relationship between money and defense?

The following processing is possible:

Mental subsystems and their subareas with the individual psychical forces:	Choose an action topic or a "critical action situation" for:
Psychodynamics	
I-Functions	
Intelligence functions	
Feelings	
Needs	
Unconscious	
Love	
Spirit: dream/meditation	

Diagram 1.2.4: The psychical network of actions

Diagramm OS2-7: Die psychischen Verflechtungen der Handlungen

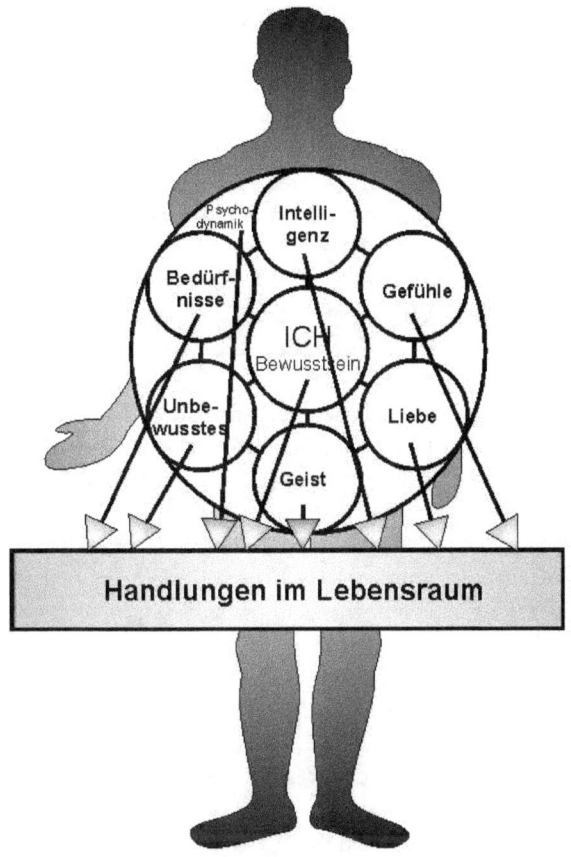

English Translation: Each psychological subsystem (Intelligence, needs, feelings, "I" / conscious, unconscious, love & spirit) with its psychodynamics affect all actions in the habitat.

1.2.5. The KES method for self-analysis

Self-knowledge also means recognizing your own actions. There are different aspects of viewing, as outlined. Actions in arbitrary situations can be broken down into different elements as well as examined in the connection with the habitat and the psychical system.

If you want to look at what you are doing for the first time, you can take advantage of small steps, looking for one dimension and then another. The result of such an analysis is always reflective and arguable. If employment is practiced with individual aspects, then one automatically gains an eye for the essentials.

The analysis of "Critical event situations" (KES) is first practiced on individual selected examples. Then there are two ways to move forward:

1) You can collect and investigate many action situations from a certain area of activity. This procedure makes it possible to fundamentally work on a sphere of life which is always up to date in the critical sense.

2) Make a list of the most important 50 KES from your own everyday life, looking back for about a month. In this way, everyone can create a profile of their general learning needs in the field of daily action.

For both ways, an analysis protocol is presented below. This can serve as a pattern of orientation to capture and analyze actions analytically.

The individual recognizes in this way of working his self-determination and self-responsibility. He also recognizes that the sum of 'critical' situations can be reduced through learning. One's own material may seem motivating.

A special challenge here is the evaluation of the value experienced. You should ask yourself, which values should you continue with.

The future-oriented view is challenging: Everybody lays the foundations for his future in some areas through his life today.

* KES in German: „Kritische Ereignissituation". Can be translated as: "Critical Event Situation". The Concept is: There is something critical and there is an event and there is a specific situation (constellation). Expertise is required to resolve all related components.

Reflection and Discussion

Three ways to analyze your own actions:

1) An action is examined for elements, dimensions, and interdependencies.

2) Through a field of activity, numerous action situations are collected and either examined according to selected criteria or recorded with a systematic analysis protocol.

3) KES is collected over all areas of life. Therefore, these are evaluated or interpreted in the overall overview according to the "KES profile".

A "KES profile" consists of four main areas:

☐ Classification of actions
☐ Classification of elements
☐ Capture of network
☐ Consequences for self-education

The analysis protocol on "critical actions" (or "critical event situations") contains the following aspects:

Analytical protocol for the "critical event situation" ('KES'):

KES indicator: General description of the event situation:

What happened?

A) Actual action in the event situation

A1 Quality of Action: What did you do? How did you do it?

A2 Objectives/intentions of the action: what did you want to achieve? What happened to your story?

A3 values in action: What is the value of the action for you?

B) Life system

B1 General context of the action situation: what was the situation?

B2 Limiting factors and influencing factors: what influenced the action of the environment?

B3 Effects in the surrounding system: What were the effects on the parts/persons in the surrounding system?

C) Acting person

C1 Self-handling of the acting person: How did you deal with yourself?

C2 Effects on the agent: What effects did the action have on you?

C3 Psychic powers (thoughts, feelings ...) of action: Which psychic powers were active?

D) Retrospective and prospective

D1 Similar event in the past: has such an event occurred earlier?

D2 Future with unchanged action: What is the future with unchanged action?

D3 Desirable act in the future: What action do you see constructively/positively in the future?

Diagram 1.2.5: The 4 dimensions of analysis of acts

Diagramm OS2-8: Die vier Dimensionen der Handlungsanalyse

English Translation: The **acting person** (Self-intercourse, agencies & inner forces) affect the **action** as well as the **critical act** (Quality, aims, values) in interplay to **time perspective** (Past, future, options) and **life system** (Situations, influences, effects).

1.2.6. Approaches and ways to change behavior

Suppose many actions are logged and analyzed. What must be done now? Different steps are possible: one can avoid the field of activity, which makes the action unnecessary. External factors may be changed. Then the situation for the plot is new.

Sometimes it is immediately apparent how the ability to change or improve a course of action is recognizable. If one wants to change one's behavior or learn new behavior, the feedback to the psychical subsystems and individual forces is indispensable. Certainly, the action will then be different in expression and experience.

Advantageously, the learning objectives are broken down into small steps. It is rarely possible to quickly change an action in a moment because the learning history is based on many hundreds of experienced situations going as far back as to childhood.

The actions are variously networked with the inner-psychic life. Therefore, it is certainly the right way, if the learning processes are understood as holistic growth processes.

This also has the advantage of a transfer effect takes place. Anyone who cultivates his perception more consciously and thinks more purposefully, considering the feelings, achieves positive effects in the most varied of action situations.

Some actions are polyvalent and have the same expression in different fields of activity. For example, someone can drive how he eats, watch TV how he deals with visitors, chat with acquaintances as well as being without his psychic life.

Realism is important: there are situations that cannot be changed, and there are actions that do not allow any other effect, even in optimal learning processes. Sometimes you must accept and live with the inevitable and unchangeable.

If you embed the analysis of critical actions in the process of individuation, then the action-oriented life changes as the tree of life grow slowly, but surely towards completely new forms.

Reflections and Discussion

Changes are possible in areas such as:

☐ Psychic organism   ☐ Context habitat
☐ Actions (Skills)   ☐ Areas of Activity (Its Components)

Learning processes include:

☐ Looking   ☐ Interpreting   ☐ Decision making
☐ Disassembling   ☐ Understanding   ☐ Setting new goals
☐ Analyzing   ☐ Recognizing values   ☐ Arousing vital interest

Creative learning, itself, contains some prerequisites that can be worked on independently of the actions.

Discuss the list below with others.

☐ I think comprehensively.
☐ I like having determination for new tasks.
☐ I am energetic.
☐ I have a realistic point of view.
☐ I give time for problem solving.
☐ I think a little ideologically.
☐ I am far-sighted when making decisions.
☐ I'm not afraid to make mistakes.
☐ I am open to learning in everyday life.
☐ I can accept unresolved issues.
☐ I am focused but relaxed in self-control.
☐ I am free from petty restrictions.
☐ I feel free from dogmatic thinking.
☐ I am not very adaptable.
☐ Situations do not need to be predictable.
☐ I am flexible in traditions.
☐ I like to develop new ideas for my everyday life.
☐ Something can captivate me.
☐ I can deal with frustrations.
☐ I also have a sense of humor.
☐ Irrationality does not make me feel so good.
☐ I look at the whole situation without losing the details.

Diagram 1.2.6: Approaches to change behavior

Diagramm OS2-9: Die Ansätze zur Veränderung von Handlungen

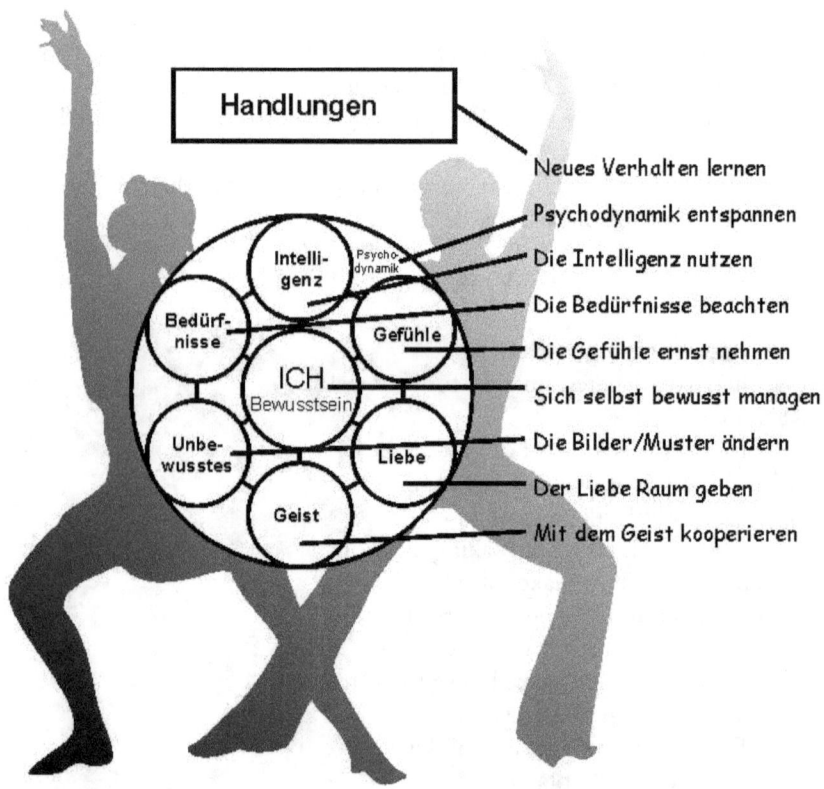

English Translation: Learning a new behavior includes: Relaxing the psychodynamic, using the intelligence, considering the needs, taking the feelings seriously, managing one's own consciously, changing images / patterns, giving love space, cooperating with the spirit.

1.2.7. Working units

1.2.7. Working unit - 1

1. a) How do you generally experience your daily actions?

1. b) Expand with your own considerations "reflecting on your own actions":

2. a) Work through the checklist; grade with "this applies to me ..."

6 = complete; 5 = very; 4 = predominantly; 3 = medium; 2 = partial; 1 = little; 0 = not

☐ My actions do not effect what I want to achieve with them.
☐ I wish that my actions will do better in the future.
☐ My actions lead to stressful situations.
☐ I do not know why I act like I do.
☐ I act without knowing what pushes me from within.
☐ I wish to understand my actions better.
☐ I experience uncertainty in my actions.
☐ I keep repeating the same actions.
☐ In different situations I want to be able to act differently.
☐ I do not think much about my actions.
☐ I cannot decide how to act.
☐ My way of acting leads to conflicts again and again.
☐ I experience myself in action without motivation.
☐ I am not very conscious in the daily routine.
☐ I experience many things that I do, as meaningless and questionable.

2. b) Total score: ....

Interpret your total score:

3. Formulate an educational goal for your actions in general:

4. a) Imagine briefly about your actions in general:

4. b) Your conclusion in one sentence:

1.2.7. Working unit - 2

1. a) How do you experience your 'critical' life themes for your future?

1. b) What are the long-term consequences of your critical life issues for your future?

2. Edit:

Components of action versus critical situation	Quality	Target / effect	Valuable Experiences
e.g. Visits			
e.g. Shopping			

3. Formulate an educational goal for your critical life topics:

4. a) What you would consider to be a critical life topic:

4. b) Your conclusion in one sentence:

1.2.7. Working unit - 3

1. a) How do you experience the interaction of these three dimensions in your life?

1. b) Extend the three dimensions with some key words:

Activities: ....

Caregivers: ....

Life System: ....

2. Examine / reflect the dimensions for each action:

Dimensions versus actions	action area	habitat	caregiver
e.g. TV			
e.g. Shopping			

3. Formulate an educational goal in the context of the three dimensions:

4. a) Imagine an aspect of one of the three dimensions:

4. b) Your conclusion in one sentence:

1.2.7. Working unit - 4

1. a) How do you experience the fact of the psychic organism in every person in your life?

1. b) Devise a consideration of the psychic organism as a "moving force":

2. Psychological forces and their expression in life. In the left column formulate examples of psychic powers and their expressions in life (keywords). In the right column extend those key words into phrases or sentences.

Mental subsystems and their subareas with the many psychical functions	Choose an action topic or a "critical action situation"
Psychodynamics	
I-Functions	
Intelligence functions	
Feelings	
Needs	
Unconscious	
Love	
Spirit: dream / meditation	

3. Formulate an educational goal for the psychic organism as a "moving force"

4. a) Imagine the interaction of the psyche with your actions:

4. b) Your conclusion in one sentence:

1.2.7. Working unit - 5

1. a) How do you experience the action analysis as a possibility of self-knowledge?

1. b) What do you see as a sense of action analysis for your future?

2. Analytical protocol on the "critical event situation" ('KES'):

Describe a situation (in keywords):

What happened?

A1. What did you do and how did you do it?
A2. What did you want to achieve, and did you achieve it?
A3. What is the value of the action for you?

B1. What was the situation?
B2. What has influenced the action of the environment around the situation?
B3. What were the effects on those within the surrounding system?

C1. How did you handle yourself?
C2. What effects did the action have on you?
C3. Which psychic powers were activated?

D1. Has such an event happened previously? (When where how?)
D2. What is the future with unchanged action?
D3. What action do you see constructive / positive in the future?

3. Formulate an educational goal for your action analysis:

4. a) Imagine winning an action analysis for you:

4. b) Your conclusion in one sentence:

1.2.7. Working unit - 6

1. a) How do you experience your learning needs in terms of behavior change?
1. b) Expand your learning opportunities with some ideas:
2. a) Edit the list below. Take note of what applies to you:

3 = predominantly; 2 = moderate; 3 = rather little

☐ I think comprehensively.
☐ I like determination for new tasks.
☐ I have a high level of energy.
☐ I have a realistic view.
☐ I use time for problem analysis.
☐ I think a little ideologically.
☐ I am far-sighted when decision making.
☐ I am not afraid to make mistakes.
☐ I am open to learning in everyday life.
☐ I can accept unresolved issues.
☐ I am focused but relaxed in self-control.
☐ I am free from petty restrictions.
☐ I feel free from dogmatic thinking.
☐ I am not very adapted.
☐ It does not have to be predictable.
☐ I am flexible in traditions.
☐ I like to develop new ideas for my everyday life.
☐ Something can captivate me.
☐ I can stand frustrations.
☐ I also have a sense of humor.
☐ Irrationality does not make me feel so motivated.
☐ I look at the whole thing without losing the details.

2. b) Total score: .... Interpret your total score:

3. Formulate an educational goal for possible behavioral changes (learning needs):

4. Your conclusion in one sentence:

1.2.7. Work unit - 7

Write a short story: "At last, people have realized that they need to change their actions. Everywhere you learn behavior change is required ...

Multiple Choice Test

Select the four correct answers:

2.1. Core elements of actions are:
- ☐ a) Goal
- ☐ b) Act
- ☐ c) Feeling
- ☐ d) Value
- ☐ e) Anticipation of expectation (effect)
- ☐ f) Duty experience

2.2. 'Critical' in the context of the actions means:
- ☐ a) Difficult
- ☐ b) Have been criticized
- ☐ c) Problematic
- ☐ d) Conflicting
- ☐ e) Emotionally stressful
- ☐ f) Wrong

2.3. Actions are networked with:
- ☐ a) Life systems
- ☐ b) Psychic system
- ☐ c) Developments
- ☐ d) Other people
- ☐ e) Quality of the action
- ☐ f) Vital energy

2.4. The following psychological subsystems affect action:
- ☐ a) I-functions
- ☐ b) Aggression
- ☐ c) Unconscious
- ☐ d) Love
- ☐ e) Psychodynamics
- ☐ f) Ability

2.5. "Critical event situations" contain as main systems:
- ☐ a) Ecology
- ☐ b) action
- ☐ c) Acting person
- ☐ d) prospective
- ☐ e) Thinking
- ☐ f) retrospective

2.6. Behavioral changes in behavior change include:
- ☐ a) Reward
- ☐ b) Analyze
- ☐ c) Set values
- ☐ d) Trying out
- ☐ e) Understanding
- ☐ f) A insight into obeying

2. Control Functions of the 'I' (Ego)

Essential theses

The ego is plagued by many internal and external forces and is in many cases overwhelmed.

Defense, habits, and 'unconscious' life replace the conscious ego control.

Each person has their own way of dealing with or repelling realities with the help functions. These are:

☐ Defense   ☐ Integration   ☐ Will   ☐ Control

The ego can only expertly control what has been taken into consciousness. For the human being, only the reality is what he has in consciousness at any time.

Man can absorb completely different realities into his consciousness. These consist of:

☐ Intrapsychic reality
☐ External reality
☐ Spiritual reality
☐ Other people

Each person has their own recorded realities that often or only partially coincide with the actual realities.

2.1. Functions to Master Life

2.1.1. The hard-pressed person

Imagine a very ordinary everyday life of a department head in a company: Mr. X, active in the finance department, 40 years old, married, three children, currently in a tense marriage, financially heavily burdened by the purchase of a house, suffers chronic insomnia, smokes a lot, and feels overwhelmed in his job.

Mr. X's day begins with the three children needing their breakfast, before going to school. His wife internally has 'terminated' the household. His sleeping pills did not work until 2 o'clock. After a business meeting that day Mr. X is supposed to go to the dentist. The shoes are not cleaned. The breakfast is not ready. The morning paper brings a headline about increasing recession. The children have exams but are still watching TV late into the night. The youngest must see the school director because of a dispute.

Mr. X does not have time for all these things. His "screen" is already full of the upcoming meeting, the tense atmosphere with his wife and a planned dinner.

Barely in the car, already in a traffic jam and the seventh cigarette is lit. He sees strange people, all driving badly and pedestrians who rush across the street. In the office, "all hell is loose". The director is annoyed. His family barely exists in the "screen". Wage reduction and part-time work are to be discussed. Incoming orders have fallen. His secretary suffers from migraines.

He goes for lunch with a colleague. Many people crowd around small tables. The air is full of the usual stink of the kitchen, smoke, and perfume. The two talk about money, cars, holidays, women, and football.

Then hard work until after 8 pm. His secretary worked late for a customer. At 9 pm he has the rendezvous that he never talks about. He comes home after midnight.

Daily balance: 35 phone calls, thirty letters, ten faxes, four meetings, one long business meeting, longing for a "problem-free" relationship, thinking about world affairs, sports and money, continuously smoking cigarettes and suffering with a toothache.

He comes home, 'caught' another action movie on Channel 9, then an advertisement about South Sea vacation. Finally, he goes to bed and takes sleeping pills.

☐ At the age of 20, most people think: this never happens to me.

☐ At the age of 30, the first young people experience approaches to such an everyday life.

☐ At 40, some are in the middle of it, fighting through, some in style, others less.

Some people break. They did not live the love and did not find it. They do not know that dreams are important, and their unconscious remains a 'darkroom'.

Reflections and Discussion

The system model of the psychic life and the model of the living space show that the ego, as the controlling authority, has much to do.

Many forces affect people daily:

☐ From the inside   ☐ From the outside   ☐ From other people

If man does not comprehensively integrate and elaborate his psychic life and outer life, live with intelligence, mindfulness, and love, then he must resort to simplifying solution patterns. These include:

☐ Renouncement of love (or reduction of self-interests) and spirit
☐ Reduction of thinking, judgment, and deduction to a minimum.
☐ Suppression and devaluation of feelings (one's own and of others).
☐ Meaning and value orientation on the scale of the "least effort".
☐ Reduction of responsibility to the most necessary and personal.
☐ Solidarity only where it serves its own interests.
☐ Increased projections: the others are the threatening inferiors.
☐ Clinging to prejudices and dogmatic or ideological teachings.
☐ Substitutional gratification and orientation to the external (material).

The consequences of such simplifying and reducing solution patterns are:

☐ Fear   ☐ Isolation   ☐ Paralysis of creativity
☐ Feeling guilt   ☐ Inner emptiness   ☐ Self alienation
☐ Aggression   ☐ Futility   ☐ Replacement behavior

This results in four basic problems or basic questions:

☐ How can the ego process all these forces and still act rationally after the assessment?

☐ What decision-making freedom does man have with this abundance of influences?

☐ What creative freedom in the sense of self-realization does the individual have in this power structure?

☐ What control options are available to man under the pressure of these forces?

Diagram 2.1.1: Forces pressing the "I"

Diagramm OS4-1: Kräfte, die das Ich bedrängen

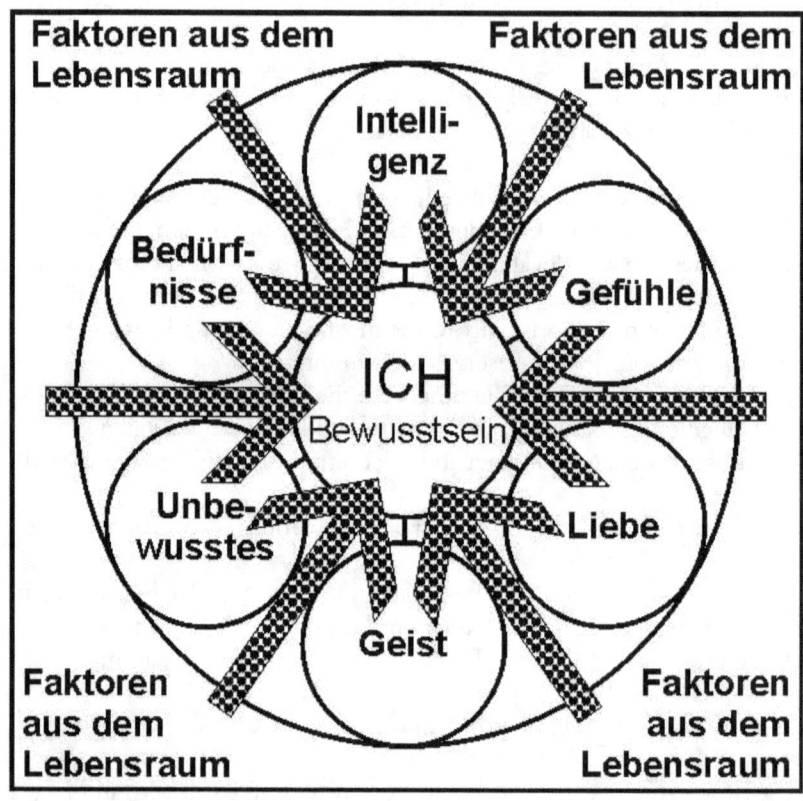

English Translation: Different factors from the living space influence the "I" and the conscious in many ways.

Sociological questions about leisure

Our key question is: How do the leisure activities affect the psychic organism of the individual? The answer requires first to form a picture of one's own pastimes. The list below gives a systematic overview.

Mark what is important to you. Include a keyword on how this recreational activity affects you.

☐ Going to the cinema
☐ Going to sports events
☐ Running or jogging in the forest
☐ Walking in the countryside
☐ Cycling
☐ Window shopping
☐ Driving around by car
☐ Visiting someone
☐ Receiving visits at home
☐ Meeting with others
☐ Going out for dinner
☐ Attending dance events
☐ Looking around the bookstore
☐ Visiting exhibitions and galleries
☐ Going to a nightclub
☐ Hiking
☐ Going to the pub
☐ Travelling over the weekend
☐ Going to a cafe
☐ Having a shopping spree
☐ Making a phone call
☐ Reading the daily newspaper
☐ Reading magazines
☐ Reading novels or entertainment literature
☐ Reading / studying books with expertise
☐ Listening to classical music
☐ Listening to light music
☐ Playing slot machines
☐ Playing computer games
☐ Writing a diary
☐ Writing letters to friends / acquaintances
☐ Attending general educational courses
☐ Participating in professional training
☐ Making renovations in the apartment

- ☐ Attending self-education courses
- ☐ Being sporty
- ☐ Playing an instrument
- ☐ Going to a disco
- ☐ Handicrafts, needlework, knitting
- ☐ Playing with a railway set
- ☐ Collecting
- ☐ Joining an association
- ☐ Painting, pottery
- ☐ Watching a video / movie
- ☐ Watching porn (movies, magazines)
- ☐ Watching television for reports
- ☐ Watching television for light entertainment.
- ☐ Watching television for sports
- ☐ Going to church
- ☐ Going to the theatre
- ☐ Reading novels
- ☐ Reading modern literature
- ☐ Reading psychological literature
- ☐ Reading philosophical literature
- ☐ Attending political events
- ☐ Viewing adverts
- ☐ Organizing festivities or attending them
- ☐ Practicing relaxation training
- ☐ Meditating
- ☐ Reading in the Bible
- ☐ Specialist cooking
- ☐ Cleaning
- ☐ Lazing around and doing nothing, or just hanging out
- ☐ Gardening, cultivating flowers
- ☐ Taking care of pet(s)
- ☐ Speaking with partner / friend
- ☐ Dealing with dreams
- ☐ Making your own biography
- ☐ Going for therapy
- ☐ Chatting with neighbors
- ☐ Listening to the radio
- ☐ Making your home nice
- ☐ Waiting around until something happens

What do your leisure activities do for you in the overall overview?

Europeans today and in the future have the following free time (as a lifetime):

- ☐ 6 hours a day
- ☐ 2.5 days a week
- ☐ 6 weeks per year
- ☐ 15 years per life
- ☐ 8 hours a day
- ☐ 3 days a week
- ☐ 12 weeks a year
- ☐ 25 years per life

Develop a vision of your life project for your free time.

Notes and Perspectives

What is the purpose of a clear understanding of the many forces that affect man daily?

Write down the key words in this subchapter:

What effects do general leisure activities have for humans?

Reflecting on the "troubled everyday life" is essential because: ...

What did you learn about the importance of free time at home, school, and church?

What significance does the conversation about leisure have in living together?

How is the decision-making space of people in politics and business reflected?

What does advertising convey about solutions for the afflicted person?

Formulate an important question for you to deal with the many influencing factors:

2.1.2. The "I" and its control forces

What is reality in the living world, becomes reality for man through his consciousness. This presupposes perception, leads to thought processes and the linguistic construction of experiences. The "I" acts in this process: "I want ... I wish".

Man sets goals and imagines his plans. Even before the question of will arises, the self can ward off: "I do not want to see that, I do not want to hear, I do not want feel, I do not want think".

In the conscious, the actual reality is constructed so that it is more pleasing to the self and closer to its interests. The facts can be twisted and deleted.

Sometimes it is too late to change the perceived. Then the "I" can negate or displace. A barrier is being built: the real reality cannot go back into consciousness.

The opposite process is integration. The "I" is open to real perception and fundamentally affirms reality as it is. A real relationship is established for reality.

The "I" can always decide which inner and outer reality is taken up. Thus, the 'I' consciously makes decisions repeatedly, which may come into consciousness. "I do not want to see this, and I do not want to know it" does not have to mean that it is a defense. For it is not always about the negation of reality, but often about self-control in consideration of responsibility and duty.

If the will for integration and employment is shaped by a certain reality, then the ego can control its psychic processes: perceiving, thinking, and acting. This includes attention and concentration, steering and management of the processes. What does the "I" do? The result will again be the subject of consciousness. This is feedback.

There are two levels in this entire process:

The reality as it is; and the reality, the self would like to have. Both aspects can affect the ego. Reality presents challenges.

It is often exhausting and stressful to see and take seriously the different realities of ourselves and others as they are. For the sake of relief, the self likes to mix reality with a desired image. With time, it is almost impossible to distinguish what is real or desired reality in consciousness.

It should be remembered that the repressed and negated always imposes itself in another form, for example: What one does not want to see in oneself, one sees in others; What you do not integrate, forces itself violently.

Reflections and Discussion

The self is to a certain extent the captain of one's own psychic life ship. Its central functions are:

☐ The defense mechanisms   ☐ The will
☐ The power of integration   ☐ The controller

The ego can keep reality away through defense, repression, and regression:

☐ Denial   ☐ Projection   ☐ Retreat
☐ Rejection   ☐ Disfigurement   ☐ Fixation
☐ Devaluation   ☐ Simplification   ☐ Shift

The integration function consists of:

☐ Affirmation   ☐ Consideration   ☐ Mediation
☐ Affection   ☐ Establish relationship

Aspects of the will are:

☐ Wanting   ☐ Pursuit   ☐ Intent   ☐ Plans
☐ Wishes   ☐ Interest   ☐ Aims

The human being also experiences the self as what he is or means to be. He has an experience of himself and information about what is all part of him: "That's me"; and expanded: "I want to be that".

The awareness of oneself is related to the awareness of other people: "Those are the others" and "That should be the others".

The awareness of oneself and others is framed in the consciousness of everything external to the living space and the "spiritual" (religious, ethical, philosophical).

The controller is the function that executes:

Regulation	Guide	Concentration	Feedback
Steering	Enforcement	Attention	

Diagram 2.1.2: The "I" and its control forces

Diagramm OS4-2: Das Ich und seine Steuerungsmechanismen

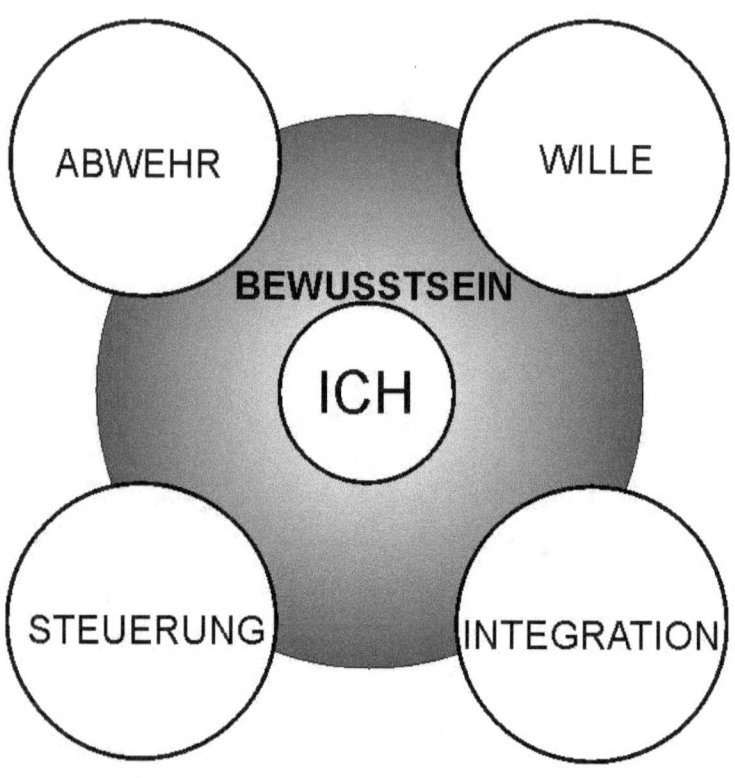

English Translation: The four control forces of the "I" are: Defense, will, controls /guidance, integration

In search of the "I"

"Who am I?" opens up different considerations, depending on how 'I' is defined. In the following, we want to present some fragments of the term 'I' so that the self-reflection in these horizons can be extended.

In everyday language, 'I' represents many meanings. These include:

- ☐ I think, I feel, I decide, I want, I act, I love, I search, I am free
- ☐ I am sick, I am different (to you), I am getting older, I am sleeping,
- ☐ I do not know who I am ..., I am travelling, I am going on vacation

Psychological view:

The "I" is the conscious-awake human being, who knows about himself, experiences himself as attuned, directed, perceiving, wishing, needy, driven, longing, feeling, thinking, acting in the continuity of his life story.

Psychoanalytical view:

The "I" can also be unconscious. An individual is now for us a psychical id, unrecognized and unconscious, to which the "I" sits on the surface, developed from the system of perception as the core.

The "I" represents what one can call reason and prudence, as opposed to the id which contains the passions. The "I", in relation to the id, resembles the rider who is supposed to restrain the superior power of the horse.

Within the "I" it must be differentiated between the ego ideal and the superego.
The ego's task is to establish a relationship with the outside world, to the id and to the super-ego, to mediate and to cope with demands and dangers.

Philosophical point of view:

The "I" is the pole on which all states of consciousness are oriented. So that "I" can become, you are a necessary condition. The extinction of the self is the highest. The "I" is a unitary point of reference, the last carrier, and active source.

"I"-ideal:

The "I"-ideal is the model that is set up inside to measure all its actions and qualities. This "I"-ideal assumes the most important functions of reality testing, of moral conscience, of self-observation and dream censorship. It is also the power that is at work in creating the 'unconscious repressed'; therefore, important to neurosis.

The identification process of the "I":

Objects of the world are pictorially 'incorporated'. In other words, they are 'introjected', and their qualities are annexed and attributed to their own self.

The Self is not the "I":

Intellectually, the self is nothing but a psychological concept and a construction that we as such cannot grasp. The 'self' (reflexive) is what man experiences as belonging to himself. But the 'self' could just as well be called 'the God in us'.

The False Prince – Or, 'The "I" that wants to be another ego' (heavily shortened and taken from: W. Hauff. Märchen, München 1994, p. 130-160).

Once upon a time:

Once upon a time there was a respectable tailor's journeyman, Labakan. He could do a pretty fine job. Often, he sat deeply immersed. There was something so special in his face and nature. His mother said, "Labakan has his noble face again". Followed by: "A prince has been lost to you." Labakan was pleased, "Did you notice that I've been thinking for a long time?" Labakan was a good person.

One day Selim, the sultan's brother, sent a dress to be changed. In secret, Labakan put this on; it suited perfectly. "Am I not as good a prince as one?" He wondered. He could not help but think that he was an unknown king's son himself. As such, he decided to travel the world with the dress. On the journey he met the young Omar, who accompanied him.

He learned from Omar: The prince's son is sought. His proof is the dagger. Omar owned said dagger.

Enraged that the other man is a true prince, Labakan planned to steal the dagger, which was the emblem of the returning prince. But he did not dare to kill him.

So, he stole the dagger and set out in a hurry to be accepted as the true prince. The dice were thrown, he could not undo what had happened, and his self-love whispered to him that he looked handsome enough to imagine himself as the son to the mightiest king.

On the hill, six men stood around an old man, who adorned a splendid dress and glittering jewels: a man of wealth and dignity. Labakan approached him, handed the dagger with the words, "Here I am, whom you seek." And the King said with tears of joy, "Blessed be the prophet who received you, embrace your old father, my beloved son Omar."

Then a rider with a horse appears on the hill. The real prince Omar is coming. The evil spirit of the lie had once driven in Labakan, so he decided, with an iron forehead to assert his rights. But Omar shouted, "Stop! Do not be fooled by the shameful cheater, my name is Omar."

Deep amazement moved the round. The old man seemed very struck. Labakan spoke with a hard-won calm: "Most gracious lord and father, do not be deceived by this man, for, as far as I know, he is called a mad tailor-journeyman from Alexandria. His name is Labakan. He deserves more our pity than our wrath."

The real prince was furious. And the king said, "Truly my son, the poor man is mad." Prince Omar exclaimed, "My heart tells me that you are my father and with memory of my mother, I swear to you, listen to me! "

The unfortunate prince is tied up. The sultan is exceedingly pleased with the figure and dignified conduct of his "son." All people cheer him, praise God, who has sent such a beautiful prince to them. Omar, the real prince, was in despair.

At home, the mother was waiting for the sultan, who had not seen her son since the birth. But she had meaningful dreams that showed the long-awaited prince that she could recognize him from a thousand faces. Presenting to the prince, she exclaimed, "This is not my son! These are not the traits that the prophet has shown me in the dream." Then Omar rushed in, prostrated himself breathlessly before the throne, " Here I want to die! Because I no longer tolerate this shame. "

The mother called, as the guards wanted to lead him away, "Stop this. This is the one my eyes have never seen, and which my heart has known!"

The sultan, quite angry, exclaimed, "I have to decide here, and here one does not judge according to the dreams of the women, but after certain, unmistakable signs! This is my son, for he brought me the dagger."

"He stole it," Omar shouted, "my naive trust he has misused to betray you!" But he is led away.

The sultan consulted with her trusted slaves. The old wise Melechsalah found a delightful way to catch the swindler, and she whispered the secret into her mistress's ear. The sultan approved.

Both should compete to see who can make the best kaftan. They received silk, scissors, needle, and thread. - A masterpiece was presented by Labakan, who was immensely proud. Omar, unable to do so because he had never learned how, could not present anything. And so, he was recognized, "Oh, you are my real son!" Cried the sultan.

In the second test, Labakan chose the box labeled "Happiness and Wealth." The real prince chose those with the inscription "Honor and Fame".

In Labakan's box was thread and needle. In Omar's a crown and scepter. The sultan crowned his real son and said to Labakan: "Cobbler stick to your last!" And he gave him his miserable life.

Notes and Perspectives

What is the benefit of good, efficient control?

Write down the key words in this subchapter:

What does a weak "I" cause?

Reflecting on what the "I" takes up (integration) is essential because: ...

What did you learn about the defense functions in your parents' home, school, and church?

What meaning in living together has the conversation about the self-assessment of the own "I"?

Which "I"-ideals exist in politics and economics?

What does advertising convey about "I"-ideals?

Formulate an important question for the "I"-control:

2.1.3. The consciousness and the reality

Man manages his life in alignment with the reality in his consciousness. If he does not see his unconscious, he rarely turns his attention to the unconscious of others.

If man does not pay attention to his feelings, then he can barely adequately grasp this with his wife.

If a person does not perceive their dreams and thus assigns them no meaning, then he misses a reality for which there is substitute: ideology, philosophy, religion.

If the human being has only the facade of outer reality in his consciousness, then he thinks about it in this superficial way.

Everything that man receives into his consciousness, during the course of life, is so to speak, the net with which he captures all other realities. What does not fit in there is not perceived, repressed, or disfigured.

What is really in the consciousness? Who checks whether what he sees and hears really corresponds to reality?

The external realities are often presented with masks or facades. An acquaintance may be known as having a positive nature, although he constantly experiences hopelessness.

The life partner never talks about problems experienced inside; therefore, he has none! Needs are admitted to consciousness only as far as they are socially accepted.

This is how some people react: "I have no problems". Because a troubled reality must not exist. What should not be allowed in a person's social network?

The further man is removed from the desired ideas of others, the more inclined he is to present himself as he is required. This happens with clothes, goods, car, career, money and with the adjustment of their own settings.

What reality is in the consciousness determines the social pressure.

This creates "life lies". The auxiliary function of the defense has much to do. These include: negating, twisting, glossing over, and suppressing.

Man has little awareness of the psychic life. Most people do not want to look closely at how their ego copes with life.

The tendency to externally harmonize ("that is all not so important and not so bad") may relax the situation in the moment.

Constructive solutions cannot be created based on this. For the unperceived reality that exists and works from within and from outside, from oneself and from others.

Like a flood, unseen reality floods the individual and the collective. This results in: suffering, social conflicts, crime, environmental destruction and in wars.

Reflections and Discussion

The reality that people have daily in their consciousness contains some salient features:

- ☐ Large space takes on its own external reality of life.
- ☐ External appearances take up more space than the psychic life.
- ☐ The space for movement of one's life comes before larger living spaces.
- ☐ The moment, the hour and the day are overwhelming time frames.
- ☐ The recorded reality tends to be 'coarse'.
- ☐ Lust-oriented values have priority over 'higher' values.

If we imagine the consciousness as a 'screen' and assume that this screen always remains the same size, then this results in:

The perceived reality is experienced as the actual reality, no matter how much is captured in the screen in space and time dimension.

There are many realities, all of which are differently captured in the consciousness of people in their differentiation. These include:

Your own external life	Your own extended living space
The foreign external life	The global living space
One's own inner life	The reality of one's own meaning and values
The foreign inner life	The religious reality

The 'I' is predominantly oriented towards the realities that have become conscious.

The unperceived reality cannot be integrated into one's way of life.

This results in various problems in all forms of actions. These include:

☐ Communication   ☐ Conflict resolution   ☐ Political life
☐ Troubleshooting   ☐ Relationships   ☐ The economy

The psychic-spiritual realities of man, and the psychic organism, are limited in consciousness.

Man is much more than he generally perceives himself to be or what others perceive.

Diagram 2.1.3: The realities in the consciousness

Diagramm OS4-3: Die Wirklichkeiten im Bewusstsein

Die wahrgenommene Wirklichkeit ist:

oberflächlich, grobförmig einseitig, emotional, subjektiv wertend erlebt und interpretiert sprachlich vage und mehrdeutig

Die wahrgenommene Wirklichkeit ist:

gründlich, detailliert, vielseitig, ausgewogen, emotional relativiert, sachlich wertend interpretiert, sprachlich klar und eindeutung

ICH

Zuerst wird wahrgenommen:

die eigene äussere Wirklichkeit die äusseren Erscheinungen der eigene Lebensraum die eigenen Interessen die Stunde, der Tag die Werte der Lust der Moment

Sekundär wird wahrgenommen:

die fremde äussere Wirklichkeit die psychische Wirklichkeit die fremden Lebensräume die Werte des Geistigen die fremden Interessen die Vergangenheit die Zukunft

English Translation: The **perceived reality** is: Superficial, coarse, partial, emotional, subjective, valued lived & interpreted, linguistically dim & plurivalent **or** Precise, detailed, all-round, balanced, emotional modified, objective valued interpreted, linguistically clear and explicit. **First perceived:** The own external reality, the external phenomena, the own habit, the hour, the day, the values, the lust, the moment. **Secondary perceived:** The foreign external reality, the psychological reality, the foreign habitats, the values of the spiritual, foreign interests, the past the future.

Transpersonal and border-psychical realities

What man does not have as realities in his consciousness is also not available to him for self-control. He lives outside of realities unknown to him. Pure fantasy is an image constructed internally, or a transcendental reality, which is beyond question.

Generally, there are scams to be found within the fields of: parapsychology, astrology, spiritual healing, and esotericism.

LSD research is just at the beginning. Too difficult are the questions of whether what appears as inner realities can also be called a transcendental reality. Nevertheless, we can point out in passing that there are many more realities than are generally perceived. These realities are:

☐ Embryonic and fetal experiences
☐ Ancestral experiences
☐ Collective and racial experiences
☐ Evolutionary experiences
☐ Experiences of past incarnations
☐ Clairvoyance, clairaudience, telepathy, precognition
☐ Time travel, repatriations
☐ Experience of dual unity (in relationships)
☐ Identification with other people and with groups
☐ Identification with animals and with plants
☐ Oneness with life and with creation
☐ Awareness of inorganic matter
☐ Planetary consciousness, extraplanetary consciousness
☐ Body exit, out of body experience
☐ Organ, tissue and cell awareness
☐ Spiritism and media experiences
☐ Experiences of encountering superhuman spiritual entities
☐ Experiences of other universes and encounters with their inhabitants
☐ Archetypical experiences, archetypal mythological experiences
☐ Experiences of meeting deities
☐ Intuitive understanding of universal symbols
☐ Activation of the chakras and awakening of the serpent power (Kundalini)
☐ Consciousness of the universal spirit
☐ Supra-cosmic emptiness

Border-psychological (para-psychological) phenomena greatly exceed the general, 'ordinary' understanding of reality of everyday consciousness. We mention some keywords: stigmatization, paranormal healing, levitations, light phenomena, life without food, telekinesis, etc.

Conclusion: We believe that most of these realities and abilities are irrelevant to personality development and individuation. On the other hand, the experiences of psychic energy, dreams, and imagination (meditation) open doors to realities that make a new image of mankind and a new understanding of life on earth possible and indeed indispensable. The 'enlightenment' about the realities of psychic life has barely begun!

Facts and patterns of interpretation

Man does not simply have 'facts' in his consciousness. Consciousness is predominantly an interpreted reality. This is called "patterns of interpretation".

"Patterns of interpretation" means:

- Stereotypical views and stereotyped interpretations
- Interpretation takes place by dealing with experiences
- From the core, concrete thinking results in a linguistically worded world
- These are more or less time-stable (patterns that repeat themselves)
- These are developed both biographically and socially.
- About everyday affairs, situations, relationships, and yourself
- Characterizing one's own identity and ability to act

Interpreting patterns have far-reaching significance. For example:

- People act because of the meanings they give to the facts.
- The criterion of what people believe to be true is in humans.
- Interpretation patterns can be learned, revised, reflected, optimized.
- Confidence in the power of one's own interpretation patterns.
- Interpretation patterns are part of everyday routine and knowledge.
- Interpretation patterns have a subjective plausibility that provides certainty.
- The current and former acquaintances affect subsequent interpretations.
- Everyone has their own 'feelings' of how 'things' develop.
- The interpreted world in consciousness tends to be a 'simplified' world.
- The interpretations incorporate subjective everyday theories.
- Uniqueness is often generalized by abstraction.
- Interpretation patterns are usually also an image of social consciousness.
- Behind the surface of formulated reality lies the deeply rooted biography.

- Biographically significant experiences form the interpretation patterns.
- In interpreting, complexity must be reduced to make actions easier.
- Prejudices and random opinions flow into interpretations.
- Interpretation patterns filter reality.
- Interpretation patterns have a certain continuity and stability.
- Rewriting is difficult as everyone 'retouches' their biography.
- Selecting and accentuating interpretive patterns.
- Discontinuity of interpretive patterns threatens self-identity.
- Patterns of interpretation acquired early in life become very sustainable.
- The correction of world views and normative orientations is difficult.
- The reorganization of interpreted inner realities is complex and not easy.
- In interpretation, man avoids inner dissonances, thus correcting reality.
- Interpretation patterns are individual, but are shaped by the environment.
- There are "group-typical" (social-layer-specific) interpretive patterns.
- Interpretation patterns have a protective function (continuity of identity).
- Interpretation patterns often develop through pressure to adapt.
- Interpretation patterns also arise from experience with one's own actions.
- Fundamental identity crises call for the correction of interpretive patterns.

Patterns of interpretation:

1) "I have repeatedly failed in my life."

2) "My background did not allow me any professional and private development."

Notes and Perspectives

What is the benefit of thinking about your own content of consciousness?

Write down the key words in this subchapter:

What does a superficial, one-sided, and emotionally perceived reality do?

Reflecting on interpretive patterns is essential because: ...

What did you learn in the home, school, and church about the relationship between reality and what is in consciousness?

What meaning, in living together, does the conversation have about the way people interpret facts and experiences?

Which facts are of importance in politics and business?

What does advertising convey about the collective reality?

2.1.4. Exercises

1. How do you experience your psychic forces in interaction with the external influences?

2. How do you manage the interplay of mental and environmental factors?

3. What aspects of you and the environment do you find enjoyable?

4. What do you take in from other people in your consciousness?

5. What of you, of others and of the habitat do you tend to ward off?

6. In which areas do you experience your will to be strong and to be weak?

7. If you have something spiritual (religious) in your consciousness, what is it?

8. What external realities occupy significant space in your consciousness?

9.a) Describe your willpower:

My strengths are:

My weaknesses are:

9.b) Describe your typical defense pattern:

My strengths are:

My weaknesses are:

9.c) Describe your ability to integrate:

My strengths are:

My weaknesses are:

9.d) Describe your self-control:

My strengths are:

My weaknesses are:

10. Empowerment = Structural and networked strengthening in the direction of a performance.

Look for your shortcomings in empowerment in the workplace and when living together with a life partner / friend. Tick what you are working on below.

Information:

3 = pronounced positive / strong
2 = moderately positive / pronounced
1 = weakly positive / pronounced

☐ Working conditions
☐ Working atmosphere
☐ Support plans
☐ Renewal
☐ Optimism
☐ Participation
☐ Company profile (identification)
☐ Leadership and insertion, leadership potential
☐ Training
☐ Consulting / Coaching
☐ Meaning, contribution to the quality of life
☐ Motivation, empathy and optimism, and goal-taking
☐ Variety, versatility
☐ Information,

- ☐ Challenging
- ☐ Self-employment
- ☐ Ideas, goals and visions
- ☐ Wages and benefits
- ☐ Company success, personal success
- ☐ Teamwork
- ☐ Partnership
- ☐ Recognition of services
- ☐ Participation, cooperation
- ☐ Clear field of application
- ☐ Flexible company goals, flexible work goals
- ☐ Loyalty
- ☐ Personal appreciation
- ☐ Business philosophy, philosophy of life
- ☐ Housing conditions
- ☐ Leisure activities
- ☐ Sexual fulfillment
- ☐ Physical condition
- ☐ Lifestyle (eating, sleeping, relaxing, rhythm etc.)
- ☐ Transparency (Thing, Process, Goals etc.)

Outline three central characteristics for good empowerment:

10.a) Living together with partner:

10.b) Professional work:

Multiple Choice Test

Select the four correct answers:

3.1. The troubled person. The following statements on the topic are correct:

- ☐ a) Humans are influenced daily from the inside and outside.
- ☐ b) The more man repels internal forces, the more he projects.
- ☐ c) Suppression often has to do with inability to work.
- ☐ d) The more one is pressed, the more one tends to simplify.
- ☐ e) Despite his own biography, man has a high inner freedom.
- ☐ f) The more man avoids life obligations, the more he can realize himself.

3.2. The "I" and its control forces. The central direct control mechanisms of the ego are:

- ☐ a) Will
- ☐ b) Integration
- ☐ c) Faith
- ☐ d) Defense
- ☐ e) Control check
- ☐ f) Boldness

3.3. Consciousness and reality. Characteristic of the daily consciousness of most people is:

- ☐ a) Rough image of reality
- ☐ b) Disfigured in consciousness
- ☐ c) Emotional
- ☐ d) Experienced subjective judgment
- ☐ e) Farsightedness
- ☐ f) Clarity

2.2. The "I" and its Auxiliary Functions

2.2.1. The consciousness and its contents

Man cannot know what he has never absorbed into his consciousness. The content of consciousness is knowledge that includes every kind of information and experience.

Four ways lead to awareness. The senses, as a first way, 'gather' the information from the outside: we see, hear, feel and so on. The second way is "inner perception": to fantasize, to meditate (that is, to imagine and contemplate), to dream, to listen to oneself, to feel emotionally for inner impulses. The third way is the recourse to the memory and the fourth way is the mental processing, which leads to a new 'information' or to a changed recorded reality.

This macro-division gives four main groups of 'realities' in our consciousness. We perceive the outer real thing, partly directly with the senses, partly technically expanded with apparatus. This includes the created cultural assets, including any kind of institutions.

Then we record human reality with all sorts of interactions and structuring. We can take this reality purely outwardly, superficially mentally or comprehensively and thoroughly into the detail of the inner-psychic life, insofar as it is recognizable by outsiders.

Then we have our own psychic subsystems, which are experienced as an inner reality. Dreams are a reality experience. they give an experience of feelings and needs. Part of this experience is 'transcendental'. They contain 'contents' of a reality that are outside the psychic system.

This raises the question of whether actual inner experiences, such a transcendental reality and fantasies, can playfully create mental ideas of any kind. We encounter these inner experiences as thoughts, and thus it becomes a changed inner reality in consciousness.

All outer and inner realities in consciousness have the form of language and images, coupled with the emotional experience of meaning, value and interpretation.

What is in the consciousness does not have to be reality.

Reflections and Discussion

The reality in the consciousness is the life orientation of humans. Whatever man does gives feedback to reality in the consciousness.

The reality in the consciousness can have different qualities. These include:

- ☐ Undifferentiated or differentiated (e.g. a table: there's 100 types of tables)
- ☐ Macro or micro dimensioned (focused)
- ☐ Oversized or undersized, spatially correct or divergent
- ☐ Timely applicable or distorted / superimposed reality
- ☐ According to the actual reality or deviating from it (disfigured)
- ☐ A 'heard' and / or 'interpreted' reality by others
- ☐ A fantasized, unexperienced (not real) reality
- ☐ A mentally processed and restructured reality
- ☐ Linguistically and figuratively differentiated or simplified reality
- ☐ A reality 'colored' by emotions
- ☐ A subjective interpretation of meaning / value / meaning
- ☐ Mixing or splitting of desire and reality, being and goa.

Everyone has in their consciousness these different qualities, e.g. over:

- ☐ Yourself as a psycho-spiritual person
- ☐ The living space with all things and conditions in the systems
- ☐ Other people with their psychic organism and interactions
- ☐ Transcendence as an inner experience or as an internalized experience

Life is also: "Realizing, coping and shaping realities". The more the inner reality in the consciousness deviates from the actual inner and outer reality, the greater are the disturbances, conflicts and difficulties in the individual and between the people / groups.

Discussion: Choose an element from each realm of reality and discuss the quality variations in the group. Which elements are predominantly in the consciousness?

How are they experienced and interpreted? What potential conflicts are given by the fact that this reality of reality deviates from the actual reality?

To the four realms of reality:

a) The own psychic reality

b) Other people with their psychic reality

c) External realities

d) Teachings / reports on transcendence

Diagram 2.2.1: From the external to the integrated reality

Diagramm OS4-4: Von der äusseren zur verinnerlichten Wirklichkeit

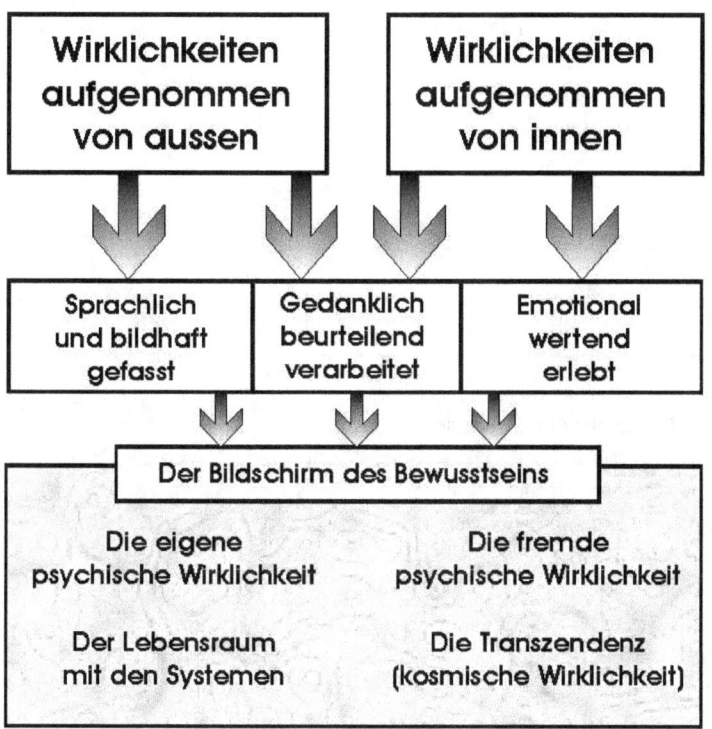

English Translation: Realities perceived from outside and from inside affect as well as linguistically and pictorial collected & processed associated valued & experienced emotionally valued the screen of the consciousness with its own psychical reality, the foreign psychical reality, the habitat with its systems & the transcendence (cosmic reality).

2.2.2. The self-living and its value aspects

Of the four main realities in the consciousness, we select the realm that man has over himself: self-consciousness. Because man is closest to himself, he is already at the location where he will encounter all other realities.

"Self-confidence" does not mean the 'size' or 'strength' that a person believes he has, but exactly according to the meaning of the word: what man has or knows about himself.

This self-confidence is always an experience that can vary daily and often every hour.

We emphasize:

Man experiences his existence: "I am here, and I am my own chance". Thus, man experiences himself with his bodily and earthly existence. This experience is the starting point for the formation of your own possibilities.

The man also experiences himself as an individual: "That's me". This includes the experience of a certain uniqueness and distinctiveness. Everything that man knows about himself is part of this aspect. As an individual, a person experiences himself as a world and a world apart: "That's me and this is you and there is the world".

And finally, man experiences meaning and value: "I am valuable, and my existence has meaning". This experience can have different qualities and vary in scope.

He who perceives himself worthless, or useless, perceives all other realities from this location. Whoever can give no meaning and no individuality to his existence creates bad foundations for life. The less man knows about himself and his psychic life, the more he sees life outside the psychic spiritual.

Those who do not experience life as a challenge with opportunities for growth and variants of world design will become sick or stunted.

The weaker man experiences himself and the less he comprehends his wholeness, the more he seeks fulfillment in compensation or illusions.

The more man is versatile and differentiated in his awareness of himself, the more he can experience interests, responsibilities, life-giving and life-respect.

If an "I" has a bad foundations it causes stagnation and regression. It will promote destructiveness and ideals that can never be fulfilled.

From this man seeks a substitute life in extreme expressions.

Reflections and Discussion

Self-living forms:

- ☐ Interests and disinterests
- ☐ Integration and defense
- ☐ Care and neglect
- ☐ Respect and recklessness
- ☐ Openness and be closed

- ☐ Mass and immoderateness
- ☐ Objectivity and impropriety
- ☐ Attention and avoidance
- ☐ Relationship and unrelatedness
- ☐ Seriousness and indifference

The less developed self-living is in quality and quantity, the more are formed:

- ☐ Substitution life
- ☐ Illusions
- ☐ Materialism
- ☐ Extremism
- ☐ Neglect
- ☐ Racism
- ☐ Misanthropy

- ☐ Compensations
- ☐ Beyond fixations
- ☐ Ego-centrism
- ☐ Dogmatism
- ☐ Meaninglessness
- ☐ Nationalism
- ☐ Sadism

Reflect on your self-living according to the following patterns:

I experience myself: "I am there"		I experience myself: "That's me"	
comprising	particulate	comprising	particulate
differentiated	undifferentiated	differentiated	undifferentiated
profoundly	superficial	profoundly	superficial
intensively	weak	intensively	weak
clear	unclear	clear	unclear
often	rarely	often	rarely

"I experience myself":

I experience myself: "You- / World-differentiated"		I experience myself: "With value and meaning"	
comprising	particulate	comprising	particulate
differentiated	undifferentiated	differentiated	undifferentiated
profoundly	superficial	profoundly	superficial
intensively	weak	intensively	weak

clear	unclear	clear	unclear
often	rarely	often	rarely

Discuss your self-living with others.

Diagram 2.2.2: Structure & consequences of self-living

Diagramm OS4-5: Aufbau und Konsequenzen des Selbsterlebens

> ## Zur Selbstbeziehung gehören:
> Interesse, Zuwendung, Wahrnehmung, Offenheit,
> Ansprechbarkeit, Verantwortung, Denken, Werterleben,
> Verstehen, Berücksichtigung, Achtung, Sachlichkeit,
> Integration, Konstruktivität, Handlungen, Mass

> ## Je weniger Selbstbeziehung, desto mehr:
> Abwehr, Lügen, Glauben, Herrschsucht, Ersatzverhalten,
> Illusionen, Projektionen, Widerstände, Unterwerfung,
> Masken, Kompensationen, Fassaden

> ## Dies hat immer Folgen:
> Leiden, Krankheiten, psychische Störungen,
> Unfälle, Aggressionen, Gewalt, Kriege

> ## Die Lösungswege setzen bei den Wurzeln an:
> Selbstbild erweitern, Abgewehrtes anschauen, Entwicklung wollen,
> Selbstbildung, Sinn und Werte finden, Zuwendung nach innen,
> Bewusstsein erweitern, alles Psychische differenziert erfassen

English Translation: Self-respect include: Interest, attention, perception, openness, receptiveness, responsibility, thinking, meriting, understanding, regard, esteem, objectiveness, integration, constructiveness, acts & mass.

The less self-respect the more: Defense, lies, faith, imperiousness, substitutional behavior, illusions, projections, resistances, subjections, masks, compensations, facades.

The consequences are: Suffering, illnesses, psychic disturbances, accidents, aggressions, violence, wars.

The approaches start at the roots: Amplifying self-perception, looking at the defensed, wanting development, self-formation, finding sense & value, care to the inside, amplifying consciousness, differentiated encompassing all psychological aspects.

2.2.3. The defensive functions and their expression

There are realities that man does not want to look at, not in himself, not in others, not in the living space and not in transcendence. Sometimes you can look away.

Often, a person must construct a mechanism so as not to look. For that there are different possibilities. The easiest way is to put something in front of it, e.g. a facade, a doctrine, a dogma, an inviolable theory.

This substitute reality must be shaped so strongly emotionally and normatively that it no longer occurs to humans to look behind it. Things get a little harder when you have seen a reality but want to push it out of your consciousness forever.

With 'forgetting' this sometimes succeeds. Override, rationalize, disfigure, perhaps even reverse the opposite, or simply invalidate the perceived, these are the mechanisms that help to repress this.

Another way is if you let the reality be; however, this is evaded by the "cannot do" delegated responsibility.

The repressed is stored in the unconscious.

The more a reality triggers fear, guilt, or frustration, the more people are inclined to ward it off. A reality can appear as a 'problem', as a challenge or danger to an already existing content in consciousness.

The more reality creates discomfort and tension, the more people tend to turn away from them.

The various defense mechanisms serve this purpose.

Sometimes this defense succeeds without damage. Often, it leads to projections that create new problems. In many cases, symptoms are the result. This is then a new reality, which in turn is rejected.

This creates frustration and aggression against oneself and others.

The realities are becoming more and more distorted in the consciousness and the attempts to solve logically fail more and more.

The inadequate mastery of reality leads to a destructive cycle.

Reflections and Discussion

What is in the consciousness depends essentially on the activity of the defense mechanism. Crucial are:

- ☐ Emotion-inducing effects of reality
- ☐ Stimulating nature of reality
- ☐ Claiming benefits to the individual through reality
- ☐ Lack of a strong foundation of the "I"
- ☐ Waiver for immediate pleasure fulfillment
- ☐ Responsibility and duty
- ☐ Social pressure, zeitgeist and social norms
- ☐ Lack of knowledge about the functioning of consciousness and defense

Defense and repression never "do away" with the defended reality:

- ☐ The defense shows itself in projections.
- ☐ Ideas of teachings are often the result of defended reality.
- ☐ Compensations and substitute behavior are symbolically same realities.
- ☐ Psychological and psycho-somatic suffering are the consequences.
- ☐ Social conflicts on a small and large scale are consequences of this.

Examples of defense or repression are:

- ☐ Avoiding problems / difficulties.
- ☐ Rejecting responsibility.
- ☐ On a small scale, constantly adapting.
- ☐ Living outwardly, which is not inside.
- ☐ Devaluing something to keep your distance.
- ☐ Sticking to principles without interruption.
- ☐ Staying defiant.
- ☐ "Forgetting" unpleasant feelings.
- ☐ Reducing meaning: "Is not bad"
- ☐ Acting, to blur the reality.
- ☐ Consumption as a substitute behavior.
- ☐ Rejection of the weak / helpless.
- ☐ Being fixated on dogmas.
- ☐ Covering against feelings of lust.
- ☐ Seeing external benefits as the highest life value
- ☐ Keeping ideologies for immutable laws

Discuss other forms of defense and repression with concrete examples:

Diagram 2.2.3: Inept reactions on the reality

Diagramm OS4-6: Ungeeignete Reaktionen auf die Wirklichkeit

Innere und äussere Wirklichkeiten bewirken:
Angst, Schuld, Frustration, Ohnmacht, Hilflosigkeit
Diese Reaktionen bedeuten:
Probleme, Gefahren, Bedrohungen, Aufforderungen

Der unangemessene Umgang mit der Aufnahme
und Verarbeitung der Wirklichkeit zeigt sich in:
1. Regressionen:
Selbstbestrafung, Selbstentwertung, Rückzug, Reduktion,
Imponiergehabe, Vernachlässigung, Isolation, Intoleranz
2. Verschiebungen:
Projektion, Identifikation, Kompensation, Umkehrung,
Agieren, ungeschehen machen, zersetzen, Symptombildung
3. Abwehrverhalten:
Abwenden, leugnen, ablehnen, entstellen, wegschieben,
vergessen, aussondern, rationalisieren

Die Rückwirkungen:
Frustration, Angst, Schuld
Aggression gegen sich und andere

English Translation: Inner and external realities cause: Fear, guilt, frustration, powerlessness, helplessness. These reactions mean: Problems, danger, threat, challenge. >
The inept handling with the perception and treatment of the reality is appears in: 1. Regression: Self-punishment, self-devaluation, retreat, reduction, display, neglect, isolation, intolerance. 2. Displacement: Projections, identification, compensation, reversing, agitation, unmaking, decomposing, forming symptoms. 3. Defense behavior: Averting, lying, refusing, deforming, brushing, forgetting, elimination, rationalizing. >
The Feedbacks: Frustration, fear, guilt, aggressions against oneself and others.

2.2.4. The integration functions (reception of reality)

Integration means: "Reception in the consciousness and admission to the treatment of this reality". Integration is based on affirmation, interest, and attention to the different realities.

Instead of being defensive, man establishes a relationship to reality. He develops more and more interest in understanding and wants to act with these and in these realities.

In this sense, integration is equal to care of life and defense is equal to avoidance of life. The integration captures the past, the present and includes the future in the present.

Care of life is open to the weak, the helpless, the undeveloped and the unpleasant. The power of integration can face the embarrassing and the frightening.

Integration results from an attitude that is conciliatory, understanding and accepting.

Integration increases to the extent that there is an interest in the inner realities, in the actual outward realities and in the human being, as they are in their psychological inner world.

Integration allows the realities to be processed and objectively comprehensively managed. Integration mediates between the "I" and the realities.

As a result, this regulatory power has much to do with love. The more the power of love is built up, the more efficient the integration becomes.

Conversely, defense and repression are predominantly based on avoiding life and hatred.

Of course, the "I" cannot allow the content of the consciousness to overflow. How could the psychological system handles such an amount?

A certain amount of regulation is needed. There is a good reason that the ego does not bring into the consciousness any reality.

What is the profit for man? Is it to look into every room, to look at any chaotic and destructive reality?

Reflected defenses and controlled integration regulate the type and quantity of the admission process.

The criterion is not denial or renouncement, but self-protection and conscious self-control for differentiation and growth.

Reflections and Discussion

Life Support is based on:

☐ Cognition interest
☐ Affirmation
☐ Establishing a relationship
☐ Acceptance of the weak
☐ Taking responsibility
☐ Realism

☐ Action interest
☐ Active attendance
☐ Willingness to engage
☐ Courage to meet realities
☐ Being understanding

The more the power of love is developed, the more the mechanism of integration can be constructive. These include, among others:

☐ Patience
☐ Interest in values
☐ Interest in the inner sense

☐ Ability to understand
☐ Protect, and to care for

Integration does not dose quantity and quality on its own, but in reference to the power of love and to the interests of one's own growth.

However, this requires a conscious self-control. If the capacity of integration is not deliberately formed, then the flood of recorded information serves to escape from oneself and to focus on lust.

Defense or integration happens by themselves. Both can and must be consciously formed. Both have an indispensable vital function for many life situations.

The defense can dose and keep away what is currently unaffordable (processable) or undesirable or experienced as harmful.

Integration can select what is conducive to mental-spiritual evolution and everyday life.

When discussing with others, make a list of what people from the realities are mostly aware of daily:

Own Reality	Other People	Habitats	Transcendence

Diagram 2.2.4: Consciousness as switch position of acts

Diagramm OS4-7: Bewusstsein als Schaltstelle für Handlungen

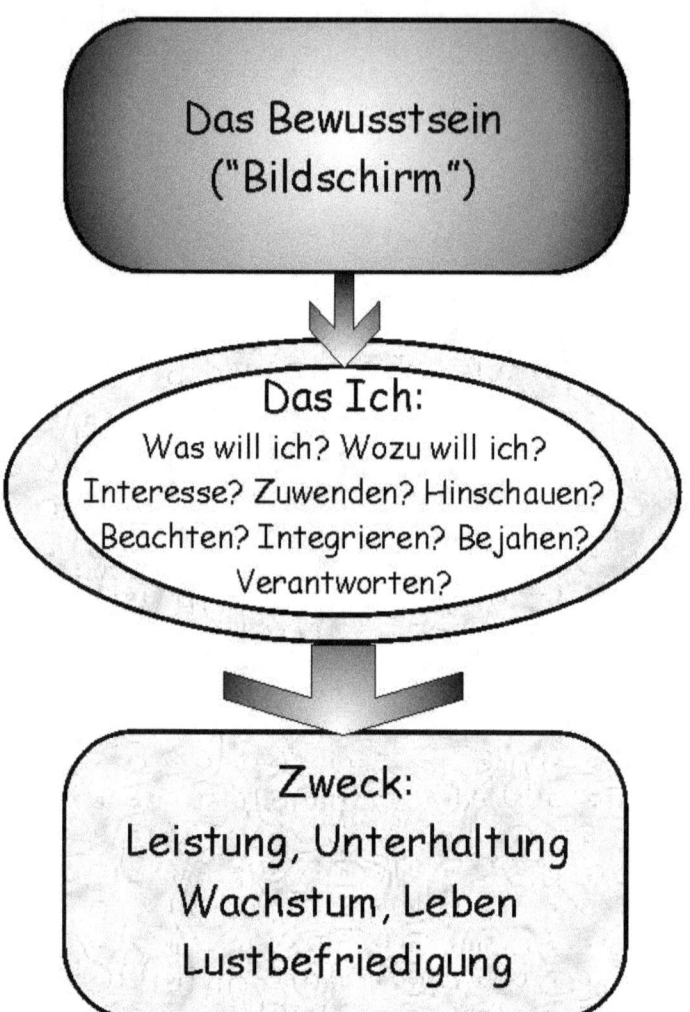

English Translation: The consciousness ("Screen")

➤ **The "I":** What do I want? What's the use for? Interest? Attention? Looking closely? Considering? Integrating? Affirming? Responsibility?

➤ **Purpose:** Benefit, entertainment, growth, life, satisfaction of lust.

2.2.5. The will / desire

When coping with life, you start with the readiness to integrate the realities. This presupposes a will, a willing. The will is a central auxiliary function of the "I". Without a will man would only function according to the instincts, habits, and influences of others.

The will is a basic building block of individual freedom. The more man unconsciously lives, e.g. does not absorb and direct realities, the more he is subject to the driving forces.

The freedom of man is never greater than his will. Life, which is not integrated into consciousness, is often stronger than existing will.

The will can be shaped, trained, and formed. Will consists of individual components: Will presupposes goals, desires, and contents. These are the result of interest and desire. The resulting action is subject to a decision. This requires the confrontation with alternatives. Thereafter, the action is targeted to activate.

Various other factors contribute to the formation of will, for example: assertiveness, role models, positive self-esteem, attention, and concentration.

Not everything in everyday life can always presuppose a conscious act of will. Some automation is essential. Habits are vital. But they also harbor dangers: habits can inhibit learning processes, render inflexible and restrict creativity. Habits often make people intolerant, promote the defense and rigid behavior.

Even thinking and responsibility can be neglected by habits. If habits are based on consciously formed will, then they are conducive and open to renewal if they no longer prove their worth.

The more the person is egocentric and has a closed awareness of the realities, the more the ability for will to cope with life is reduced.

Reflections and Discussion

Will comes about through:

Concentration	Adaptability	Thinking
Attention	Confidence	Ambition
Flexibility	Amplifier	Interest
Alternatives to comparison	Role model	Motivation

The less people consciously form their will, the more habits, pleasurable impulses, and external influences guide daily life.

Habits pose dangers. These include:

Lack of freedom	Compulsive schema
Indifference	Fixations
Unconscious lifestyle	Ground-in patterns
Defense	Self-righteousness
Rigidity	Striving for power
Learning inhibitions	Inertia

The ability to form the will is as important as reading and writing if you want to develop individuality and freedom.

It is easy to say, "I want ..." and then there are opposites pressures, where many different influences and interests collide.

The 'solution' in the sense of "erasing will" is against life and therefore not a solution. Important is the correspondence with all the different psychological subsystems, especially with love and the spirit as well as the ability to adapt the real possibility.

Break down an example from your everyday life and discuss with others:

Will	Targets	Interest	Alternative	Decision

Diagram 2.2.5: Will coming of through

Diagramm OS4-8: Wille kommt zustande durch

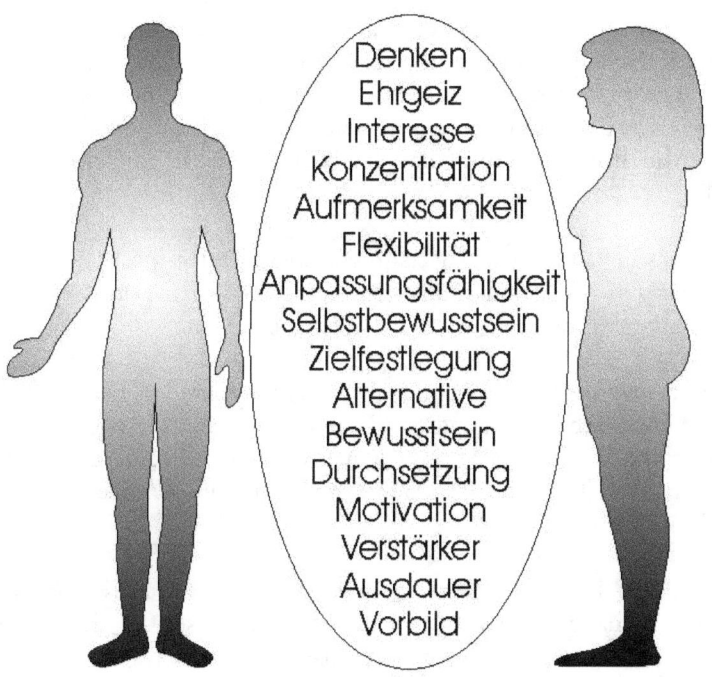

Denken
Ehrgeiz
Interesse
Konzentration
Aufmerksamkeit
Flexibilität
Anpassungsfähigkeit
Selbstbewusstsein
Zielfestlegung
Alternative
Bewusstsein
Durchsetzung
Motivation
Verstärker
Ausdauer
Vorbild

Grundsatz: Die Lösung eines Willensproblems liegt nicht im "ich will", sondern in diesen 16 Aspekten, die den Willen formen und grundlegen. Die Realisierung eines Wollens kann nicht besser sein als die psychichen Grundlagen. Die Kompromisse liegen immer im Fundament.

English Translation: Thinking, ambition, interest, concentration, attention, adaptability, self-consciousness, aim determination, alternative, consciousness, enforcement, motivation, intensifier, persistence, model.

Principle: The solution of a will problem lies not the "I want" but in the 16 aspects which form and inform the will. The realization of a desire can't be better than the psychological foundations. The compromises lie always in the basement.

2.2.6. The "I"-control

The will is determined, and the decision is made. But that is not the goal yet. In many cases in life it remains the will. The execution of the specified action requires "I"-control.

If you really want to achieve a specific goal, you must put it into practice. Actions are to be regulated, coordinated, planned, and organized. A certain concentration on the course of the action can only be beneficial for an effective action. The act itself is to be steered and, if necessary, enforced. Sometimes it is beneficial to check the steps in the direction of the goal. The effects of the process are to be coupled back to the "I"-guidance and lead to the goal.

There are several additional aspects to consider in this process of "I"-control. The habitat sets conditions and often limits. Facts and interests of other people may be contrary to the target achievement.

Then your own psychic powers must be considered. The "I"-leadership requires thinking, the consideration of the feelings, and the coordination with the inner spirit. The psychodynamics may set limits of force: Not always the captain can with "full speed" encounter the goal! He also needs to count on "storms" and "waves".

So here the "I" has the function of mediating between these forces and of achieving a balance between will and compromise. In the process of realization, perhaps new goals may be set, and other ways be taken. All this must include the self-responsibility in the "I"-control.

The "I"-control starts when awakening. Throughout the day, man can hold his life steering wheel firmly in his hands. Many let go of the steering wheel quickly and let themselves drift. Some forget the "I"-control in conversation, at dinner or at the latest in the evening in front of the TV.

Above all, "I"-guidance means "living consciously" and always codetermine in the course of events with thinking. Conscious "I"-control is also a goal and requires an act of will.

Reflections and Discussion

The main components of ego control are:

Setting objectives	Regulation	Organization
Guidance	Coordination	Decision
Giving content	Planning	Concentration
Enforcement	Control	Feedback

The formed will is important for achieving the goals, but it is also important to consider:

Interests of other	Limits of psychodynamics
Habitat conditions	The other subsystems
Unexpected events	New changed situations

Effective self-control includes:

- ☐ Ability to cooperate
- ☐ Demarcation against the outside
- ☐ Independence
- ☐ Rooting in love
- ☐ Feedback with the spirit
- ☐ Selection and weighting
- ☐ Objectivity (competence)
- ☐ Appropriate handling of situations
- ☐ Allowing developments growth
- ☐ Balance between will and location

The enforcement of an action also requires the responsibility.

Initiation	Course	Moment
Completion	Variants	Amount

Find some everyday situations for self-control:

Situation	Effective control	Weak control

Diagram 2.2.6: The "I"-control and its subfunctions

Diagramm OS4-9: Die Ich-Steuerung und ihre Teilfunktionen

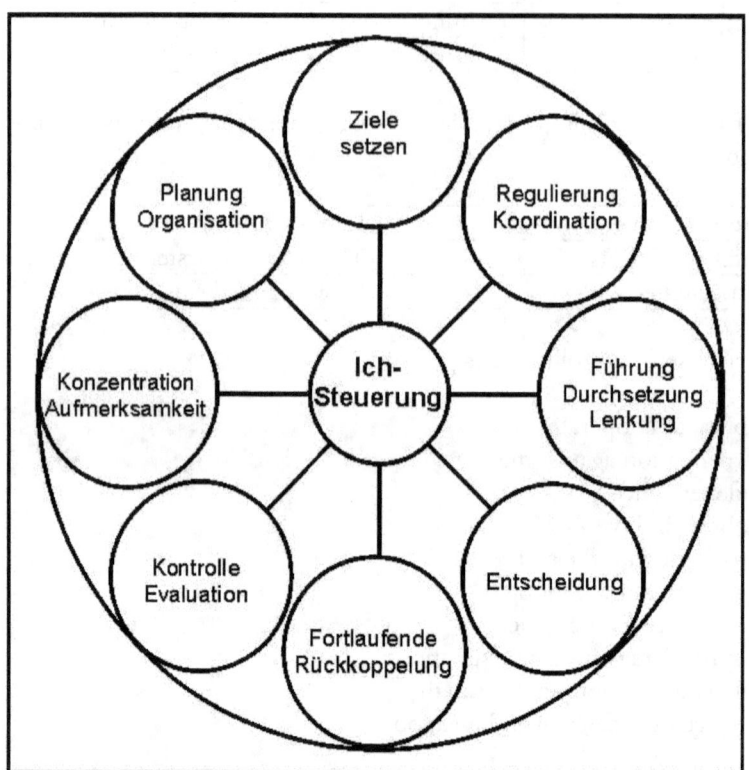

English Translation: "I"-Control is composed of: Setting aims / regulation & coordination / conduct, assertion & guidance / decision / continuous feedback / control & evaluation / concentration & attention / planning & organization.

2.2.7. Working units

2.2.7. Working unit - 1

1. a) What are the daily dominant contents in your consciousness?

1. b) Which orientations give you your own contents of consciousness?

---

2. Next, select an element from each realm and describe the quality variants for daily life. Questions about this are, for example: Which elements predominantly come into consciousness? How are they experienced and interpreted? Which potential conflicts are given by the fact that this consciousness of reality deviates from the actual reality? The four realms of reality are:

1) The own psychical reality:

2) Other people with their psychical reality:

3) External realities:

4) Teachings / Transcendence Reports:

---

2. b) What do you conclude from your information for interpersonal communication?

3. Formulate an educational goal about the qualities of your consciousness:

4. a) Imagine the tendency of your average content of consciousness:

4. b) Your conclusion in one sentence:

2.2.7. Working unit - 2

1.a) How do you experience questions about out your own self-confidence?

1.b) Extend the risks of a weak and narrowed self-image:

2.a) Reflect on your self-living according to the following patterns. Tick what applies to you:

I experience myself: "I am here"		I experience myself: "That's me"	
all-embracing	particulate	all-embracing	particulate
differentiated	undifferentiated	differentiated	undifferentiated
deeply	superficial	deeply	superficial
intense	weak	intense	weak
clear	unclear	clear	unclear
often	rarely	often	rarely

I experience myself: "You- / World-differentiated"		I experience myself: "With value and meaning"	
all-embracing	particulate	all-embracing	particulate
differentiated	undifferentiated	differentiated	undifferentiated
deeply	superficial	deeply	superficial
intense	weak	intense	weak
clear	unclear	clear	unclear
often	rarely	often	rarely

2. b) Interpret your overall picture:

3. Formulate an educational goal for you about your self-living:

4. a) What is your ideal, desired self-image?

4.b) Your conclusion in one sentence:

2.2.7. Working unit - 3

1.a) How do you experience the mechanisms of defense in humans?

1.b) Expand the potential impact of increasing displacement:

2. Present and interpret further (own) defense and displacement forms with concrete examples:
a)
b)
c)
d)

3. Formulate an educational goal to control your defense mechanisms:

4.a) Imagine your tendency to defend yourself. What is it against?

4.b) Your conclusion in one sentence:

2.2.7. Working unit - 4

1.a) How do you experience the mechanism of integration with you?

1.b) Extend the consideration of the purpose for integration:

2. Create a list of single elements of what people from the realities are mostly aware of daily:

Own Reality	Other People	Habitats	Transcendence

3. Formulate an educational goal to control integration:

4.a) Imagine your integration dynamics:

4.b) Your conclusion in one sentence:

2.2.7. Working unit - 5

1.a) How do you experience your willpower? Describe it:

1.b) Expand the topic of will with some life experiences about others:

2. Give 2 examples "I want ... and I cannot " from your everyday life:
a) 1st example:

Will	Target	Interest	Alternative	Decision

b) Example 2:

Will	Target	Interest	Alternative	Decision

3. Formulate an educational goal for you to strengthen the will:

4. a) Think of what your willpower is:

4. b) Your conclusion in one sentence:

2.2.7. Working unit - 6

1. a) How do you experience your self-control in your life?

1. b) Extend this topic with a few short critical reflections:

2. a) Describe a situation from everyday life for self-control:

Situation	Effective control	Weak control

Interpret the various aspects / elements of the controller:

2. b) Describe another situation from everyday life for self-control:

Situation	Effective control	Weak control

Interpret the various aspects / elements of the controller:

3. Formulate an educational goal in the context of the self-control sub-functions:

4. a) Think about your own self-control:

4. b) Your conclusion in one sentence:

2.2.7. Working unit - 7

Justify the thesis: Most people have no more than 5% awareness of what they are and how they live. This has a correspondingly critical effect on the self-control.

Multiple Choice Test

Select the four correct answers:

4.1. Mark the following correct sentences:
☐ a) The self-image is only part of the content of consciousness.
☐ b) The highest consciousness is the "Consciousness Void".
☐ c) Everyone has an awareness of the world (animals, nature, environment, etc.).
☐ d) Not everything in consciousness is actually a reality.
☐ e) Consciousness content is almost always easier than reality.
☐ f) "The highest Consciousness" leads to God and away from the psychic organism.

4.2. Self-awareness shapes basic attitudes, which include:
☐ a) Mass   ☐ b) Interest
☐ c) Consideration   ☐ d) Perception
☐ e) Care   ☐ f) Logical thinking

4.3. Defense functions are:
☐ a) Compensating
☐ b) Acting
☐ c) Lying / negating
☐ d) Keeping a critical distance
☐ e) Disfiguring
☐ f) Disassembling / micro analyzing

4.4. Aspects of integration include:
☐ a) Establishing a relationship   ☐ b) Taking responsibility
☐ b) Taking everything seriously   ☐ d) Interested in an action (s)
☐ c) Conflict   ☐ f) Symbiosis / Identifications

4.5. Elements of the will (act) are:
☐ a) Instinctive force   ☐ b) Expectation
☐ c) Decision making   ☐ d) Taking action
☐ e) Attention   ☐ f) Intuition

4.6. The I-control acts with:
☐ a) Planning   ☐ b) Control
☐ c) Reduce feelings   ☐ d) Enforcement
☐ e) Evaluation   ☐ f) Let go

3. Cognitive Functions

Essential theses:

Intelligence is a complex system of functions and activities consisting of:

- ☐ Perception
- ☐ Language
- ☐ Thinking operations
- ☐ Thinking learning

The perception of people is vastly varying in differentiation, quantity, types of realities, time, and value dimension.

What the human being consciously perceives, he gives linguistic labels, via words and signs. The subjectivity (meaning variety) is large.

The thinking has multiple operations and can be of different quality.

Thinking learning is a conscious intentional working process.

The more man learns thinking the better, and the better conditions he will creates for further learning and for his lifestyle.

Thinking and learning with integration of the psychological reality causes an individual deepened quality of life: Meaning and values for being human.

3.1. The Complex Functions of Intelligence

3.1.1. Intelligent processes

'Intelligence' is more than the "intelligence quotient" and what a test measure. We capture the complex system from perception to the mind-forming learning processes as an intelligent system: The consciously controlled and reflected perception, the linguistic assignment, the thinking processes, and the learning contained therein.

The result of an intelligence activity is a newly organized reality in consciousness that structures the perceived reality in a more differentiated way. Man understands better and practices more appropriately.

The perceived reality becomes a cultivated reality in consciousness through the intelligent processes.

In the thinking structuring, different levels arise: Information, value judgment, interpretation of meaning, explanation, theory, classification, systemic acquisition, experience description, instruction, desire, prognosis, threat, proposed action, and decisions.

The result is the starting point for the "I" to act via communication, and activity. The action as a result is the product of this complex intelligent process. Any form of coping with reality goes through this process.

All the steps of this intelligent process involve various other psychological powers. The needs unconsciously control the perception. Defenses forces steer the perception. Some perceived reality receives a different picture in consciousness, through "hasty" distortion.

The lived past affects attractively or repellently, always regulating the perception and the intellectual process. The Emotions significantly influence the thinking process. Through differentiated thinking, reality becomes more precise.

But again, the defense works. The "I" do not want to see the consequences of an assessment. This is how other thinking results develop. Social pressure, too, influences thinking processes if the result endangers existing positive group affiliations.

Man tends to accept and cooperate with people in his environment that think in unison and come to the same conclusions.

Thinking can have many consequences. It always has an impact on the person: Thoughts, attitudes, patterns of actions can also be questioning. New learning or relearning is required. This can cause insecurity and anxiety, "disturb" relationships, and lead to conflict with others.

That is why many people think little. Even non-thinking or wrong thinking has consequences.

Reflections and Discussion

The human being receives with the inner and / or outer perception "things" i.e. realities in the consciousness. We perceive quite different realities with different senses:

- ☐ Sight
- ☐ Being / feeling
- ☐ Inner vision / intuition
- ☐ Hearing
- ☐ Tasting / smelling
- ☐ Motional perception

Perception happens 'systemic' (holistic), identifies and organizes according to previous perceptions (patterns), even before thought processes begin.

Man gives words and signs, e.g. language, to what he perceives. Thinking processing set the assignment of terms and signs in advance. Thinking performs in language: Words and signs are combined according to certain rules, linked to culture and 'milieu'.

The question "What is truth?" above all, is also a language problem: We can grasp the same situation with different words and signs as 'good'. Moreover: Language always remains only language, it is never the reality itself.

The process of language assignment and thinking always happens in feedback with the memory. We cannot perform intelligent operations without this reference. Thus, man assigns his perceived reality to the linguistic net which he already possesses.

The extension of this network is a thinking and learning achievement. The more openly this earned ability to perform is practiced, the more the human being continually expands his reality in the direction and extension of the effective reality. There are various thought processes, including:

- ☐ Producing similarities / analogies
- ☐ Disassembling / reassembling parts
- ☐ Understanding relations
- ☐ Allocating meanings
- ☐ Target-oriented processing
- ☐ Classifying
- ☐ Abstraction of space and time
- ☐ Combining and comparing
- ☐ Capturing causes
- ☐ Assigning values
- ☐ Concluding

The way in which intelligent thinking operates are used can lead to learning results:

➤ New insights, New goals, New values, New actions, New plans

Diagram 3.1.1.: The intelligent main-functions

Diagramm OS5-1: Die intelligenten Hauptfunktionen

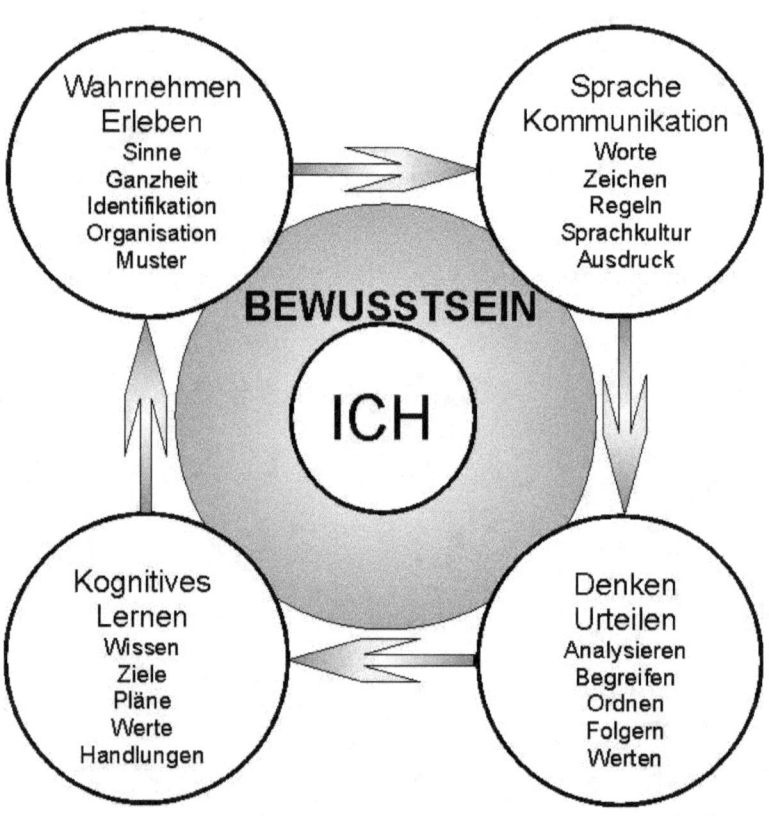

English Translation:
Perception & experience: Senses, entity, identification, organization, patterns
Language & communication: Words, signs, rules, language culture, expression
Cognitive learning: Knowledge, aims, plans, values, actions
Thinking & judging: Analyzing, understanding, arranging, concluding, valuing

Some text-study for learning techniques

Three main ideas:

1. Planning learning: Factor time, learning material, aids, goals, tasks, interest
2. Regulated learning: Setting priorities, not repeatedly edit known "things"
3. Control learning: Identifying result, remembering by summarizing

Seven learning techniques when studying texts:

1. Organize content (topics), group into areas, and create an overview:

- ☐ Initial reading: detecting gross skimming and main elements / structure
- ☐ Sketches, design models (circles, squares, connections, etc.)
- ☐ Create a keyword network (mind-mapping) after the first rough reading
- ☐ Create a file and organize knowledge elements on maps

2. Divide contents (topics) into subgroups.:

- ☐ Divide models from the beginning
- ☐ Create secondary lines in mind-mapping

3. Precise reading and filtering out of:

- ☐ Facts
- ☐ Distinction between important information the extra around it
- ☐ Difficult words (foreign words, technical terms)
- ☐ Interpretations
- ☐ Ratings
- ☐ Emotion-filled experience expression
- ☐ Explanations
- ☐ Goals, intentions and justifications
- ☐ Consequences
- ☐ Shortcuts

4. Summarize the core ideas according to suggestions 1-3:

- ☐ First in keywords
- ☐ Your own formulation of the core statements in short sentences.

5. Find your own starting points for the topics, a thesis, or thoughts:

- ☐ Practical examples
- ☐ Experiences
- ☐ Existing factual knowledge
- ☐ Identify practical applications
- ☐ Expand with your known knowledge, and attach to existing models

6. Record your flow of thoughts in a flowchart:

a) The presented thing on an abstract level

b) What is presented at a concrete level?

7. Formulate objections to individual thoughts in writing (keywords):

Learning Difficulties

(Compiled from various classical educational literature on didactics.)

- ☐ Un-lust for learning, barely invigorating or energetic forces
- ☐ Lack of motivation to learn
- ☐ Indifference, no inner sympathy with the topic
- ☐ Interests strongly tied to personally appealing sentences / thoughts
- ☐ Poorly reasoned learning: Why this? Just now? And so?
- ☐ Little desire to discover, little curiosity about something new
- ☐ Intellectually unresponsive (it must be concrete and exciting)
- ☐ Doubts about the purpose of learning.
- ☐ Started to learn by third party pressure
- ☐ Quickly lost interest, strong short-lived attention
- ☐ Somehow blocked against new things
- ☐ Negative feelings towards scientific, abstract texts
- ☐ Trust in one's own learning ability (thinking)
- ☐ Trust in one's own judgment
- ☐ Resistance to effort and discipline
- ☐ Afraid to form own opinions and theoretical hypotheses
- ☐ Little experience of what it means to take responsibility in learning
- ☐ Difficulties adjusting to new learning situations (new knowledge)
- ☐ Stress in learning / through learning
- ☐ Difficulties with concentration
- ☐ Strong cognitive-emotional orientation to dogmas

- Ideologically fixed way of thinking
- Strict, rigid superego (restricts creativity and originality)
- No stamina in abstract thinking
- Constant need for harmony (cannot stand contradictions)
- Imitating too much others, instead of thinking in your own words
- Anti-scientific attitude
- No critical distance to scientific work
- Lack of tying points for one's own actions
- Overburdened with problems and conflicts privately and at work
- Stressful experiences from one's own time at school
- Regressive reaction patterns towards teachers (and authors)
- Insufficiently considering that many authors write unclear
- Trivialization on the one hand and exaggeration on the other hand
- Cannot accept own competence deficiencies.
- Devaluing the need for life-long and life-wide learning
- Low frustration tolerance
- Never been led to the world of nonfiction
- The idea that subject-based learning is only for "intellectuals"
- Spoiled too much
- No ability to suffer in the struggle for understanding and linguistical grasping
- Internally beset by general dissatisfaction and displeasure
- Constant retention of one's own life force
- No planned use of breaks and variety
- Indecision in one's own goal and way determination
- Strong prevalence of utility thinking
- Little empathy in the different language forms of the text
- Not taking the meaning of knowledge / life seriously
- Little will to acquire new attitudes about subject areas

➤ Learning is work, a strenuous activity, and a personal challenge!

➤ Learning never stops. It is unlimited in one lifespan and lifetime!

Notes and Perspectives

How does man experience (on average) his main intelligent functions?

Write down the key words in this subchapter:

What is the effect of poorly formed functions of the intelligence?

Reflecting on learning difficulties is essential because…

What did you learn about learning techniques in home, school, and church?

What significance in living together has the conversation about thinking and judgments have?

What do you think about learning for new goals and new values in politics and business?

What does advertising convey about thinking and judgments?

Formulate an important question about learning difficulties:

3.1.2. Quality and performance differences

When people talk to each other, they realize seldom that everyone has his own reality in his consciousness. They hardly suspect that everyone experiences many words in his own way and links things that are hardly pronounced.

It is also not customary for one to thoroughly look at the thinking processes of another. Who observes in a discussion which inner psychic forces co-control talking and listening?

Man has little clear awareness of the difference between the genuine realities and the realities conveyed by words which can be interpreted in many ways, which are then reshaped in a new linguistic and intellectual way.

Thinking is working. Thinking is also a conscious willfully performed act. The quality of the performance of thinking differs much among people.

Many people rarely think, too little or incorrectly. They unreflectively connect their words with feelings, with values and with their positive or negative life experiences.

Tags and beautiful labels make dealing with reality easier and clearer. Prejudices save the differentiated exhausting thinking.

Imagine: Human 0 can neither write, nor read, nor calculate. He cannot distinguish green from red, does not know the difference between water and gasoline. Every time the vacuum cleaner runs, he has palpitations because he thinks there is a ghost inside it. Neither can he distinguish washing powder from other powders. Money is just paper for him. He cannot read the time, does not use a phone, and God blasts the lightning to earth. Human 0 would have little chances of surviving his daily life in our industrialized world.

Very few people live in relation to their psychical life and to the psychical life of their fellow human beings.

What they do not understand comes from God or the devil. What they do not grasp is unimportant. What they cannot handle is waste and useless.

One lives with what one knows: In one's own life, in political life, in matters of religion and faith. The rest is delegated: Deported into the ridiculous or evil, in dogmas or in an ideology.

Many people still feel "God's will" when a "soul is brought home" by an incident such as a traffic accident, although the causes lie with humans.

Properly and responsibly 'driving' with one's psychical organism requires educational achievement, which need to be learned.

Reflections and Discussion

Perception has different qualities. These include:

☐ Spatial dimension
☐ Time dimension
☐ Focusing and differentiation (macro-micro view)
☐ Inner and outer realities
☐ Value perception
☐ Mobility / fixation / centering

Language has many aspects with subjective dynamics:

Feelings	Objectivity	Associations
Values	Diversity	Levels of abstraction

If two people use the same words, that does not mean that they mean the same thing. In many cases, people have simple ideas about vague ideas tied to their life experiences. Many words are an interpretation of perception, for example:

Seriously	Unsympathetic	Friendly	Overbearing
Tolerant	Diligently	Digested	Necessary
Spiritually	Honest	Religious	Well

Thinking operations vary in style and in quality. Reasoning is as good as the possible operations, when used meaningfully and optimally. Sources of error start with:

☐ Perception   ☐ Assignment of words ☐ Thought operations
☐ Feeling an experience ☐ Experience of value   ☐ Resulting action

Cognitive learning requires interest and purposeful volitional thinking. Those who do not learn reproduce the previously stored patterns.

All subsystems of intelligence operate with considerable variability, varying quality, and considerable subjectivity.

Diagram 3.1.2: Subsystems of intelligent achievements

Diagramm OS5-2: Teilsysteme intelligenter Leistungen

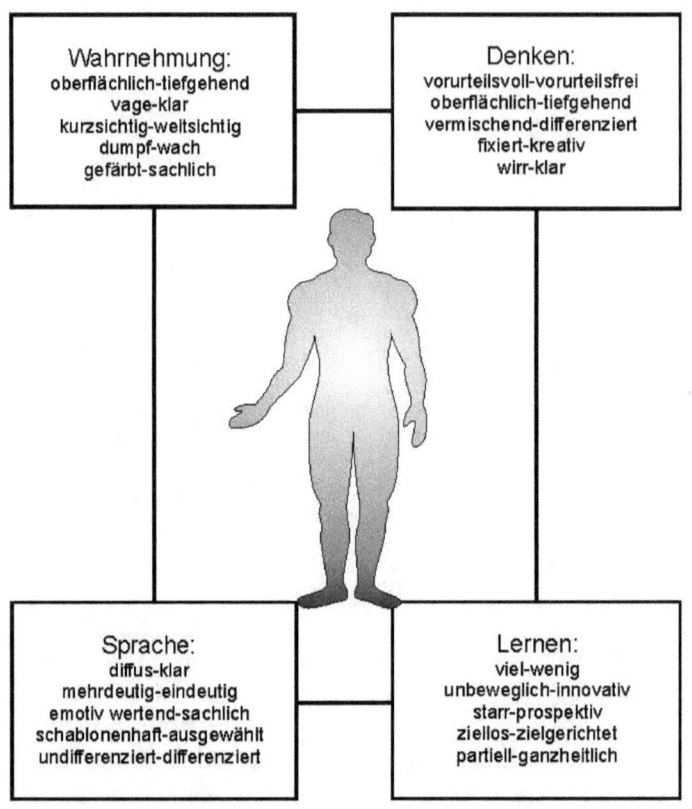

Wahrnehmung:
oberflächlich-tiefgehend
vage-klar
kurzsichtig-weitsichtig
dumpf-wach
gefärbt-sachlich

Denken:
vorurteilsvoll-vorurteilsfrei
oberflächlich-tiefgehend
vermischend-differenziert
fixiert-kreativ
wirr-klar

Sprache:
diffus-klar
mehrdeutig-eindeutig
emotiv wertend-sachlich
schablonenhaft-ausgewählt
undifferenziert-differenziert

Lernen:
viel-wenig
unbeweglich-innovativ
starr-prospektiv
ziellos-zielgerichtet
partiell-ganzheitlich

English Translation: Perception: Superficial – penetrating, vague – clear, myopic – clear-sighted, musty – awake, dyed - objective

Thinking: Full of prejudice – open-minded, superficial – penetrating, unselected – differentiated, fixed – creative, confused - clear

Language: Diffuse – clear, ambivalent – explicit, emotionally valuing – objective, cut and dried – selected, in-differentiated - differentiated

Learning: much – few, immobile – innovating, rigid – prospective, aimless – purposeful, partial – all-embracing

Intelligent interaction design

Below are some of the rules for interacting with perception, thinking, language and learning ability:

- ☐ Despite interest, no success in a bad climate
- ☐ No success without a parallel interest in success
- ☐ Orientation facilitates decision
- ☐ Reduce resistance through transparency, information, positive attitude etc.
- ☐ Emotionally strong positive aspects ('anchors') channel decision
- ☐ Pick so counterpart from where he / she stands (information, motivation)
- ☐ Dissonance in behavior is slowing down
- ☐ Dissonance in matters is threatening, slaying (i.e. targets or requirements that are too high).
- ☐ A false instant stops
- ☐ Spatial dissonance blocks (do the right thing in the right place!).
- ☐ Unfinished problems with a counterpart causes too much distraction
- ☐ Quality of a relationship determines the perception
- ☐ Prepare your interests and goals with flexibility
- ☐ "I"-messages (self-expression) promotes interaction

"Anchor" = Image, issue, word which opens in the counterpart a positive identification

'Agogic' = humans purposefully and intelligently leading, directing, and educating.

Customization options:

1) <u>Posture:</u>
- ☐ Open, defensive, easy, formal
- ☐ Breathing: relaxed, tense
- ☐ Stomach: easy
- ☐ Speech: tone, speed, rhythm, softness
- ☐ Language: keywords, words from the life experiences of the interlocutor

2) <u>Showing an interest in you (situation, thinking, needs, possibilities):</u>
- ☐ Questioning, listening, understanding signaling
- ☐ Repeating and noting the stages of memory (short term store: 10 sec.). A few words, short sentences. Note: Short-term memory: 1-2 days, 7-9 words. Long-term memory: months, but only by repetition and / or emotional anchoring.

3) Building visions:
- ☐ Easily using emotional (not too strong!) colored pictures
- ☐ Anticipating the future of the subject matter
- ☐ Constructing mental film with YOU elements
- ☐ Presenting the picture as an experience
- ☐ Pictures should be clear, colorful, positive, forward-looking, and bright.

4) Design information:
- ☐ Addressing the senses with words and pictures
- ☐ Senses: taste, see, hear, smell
- ☐ Feel warmth, touch, muscle layer, gravity
- ☐ Networked and graded designing: enable repetition

5) Serve, explain, giving orientation:
- ☐ Conceiving constructive attitudes
- ☐ Giving decision support
- ☐ Supporting emotionally
- ☐ Appellative: doing something to make something happen.

Critical to judge is:

- ☐ Enveloping others with sweet and kind words
- ☐ Creating pressure with pseudo-facts and exaggerations
- ☐ Creating illusions: Happiness, success, wealth, and healing are easy illusions to achieve
- ☐ Creating familiarity with private questions and comments
- ☐ Covering a lie with fictional frame stories
- ☐ Strengthen the other in his narcissistic feelings

Flexible and intelligent design:

- ☐ Recognizing the culture of life (creation, organization, leadership) of the other
- ☐ Understanding each other's language (keywords, facial expressions, gestures, tone of voice etc.)
- ☐ Seeing through the game of the other (mask, facade, manipulations)
- ☐ Recognizing and reducing weaknesses of the other: power talking
- ☐ Building decision-making process in terms of content and defense
- ☐ Creating safety and support where necessary (conveying information and skills)
- ☐ Recognizing and tackling resistance in the person and in their networks
- ☐ Promoting life creates a positive relationship climate: Experience, efficiency, benefit.

- Identifying an anchor allows to expand processes of decision making
- Being a life coach: Serving, helping, counseling, supporting, promoting.
- Recognizing and promoting conscious and unconscious motives, and respective needs
- Identifying instincts that create a need or a motive
- Interpreting behavior on defense, openness, and phase of determination
- Recognizing attitude to the thing / matter and positively reinforce or shape
- Remove blocking habits (behavior, feeling, perception, thinking)
- Drawing and identifying positive future orientation
- Promoting self-esteem (ego strength)
- Accepting the other as a separate personality
- Respecting arguments (not everything is arguable, rationally logically or solvable!)
- Involving the other in the conversation and allowing him to have his say
- Feelings (self-experience) and instincts are in front of the argument
- Searching and stimulating sympathy medium
- How to be: polite, friendly, fair, demarcated and sometimes serious and strict.
- Keep your goals, ideas, and suggestions flexible
- Creating 'comfort': atmosphere, mood, relaxation, active interest
- Exploring options (alternatives)
- Preparing (thinking through) important interactions (conversations)
- Step-by-step approach: noting steps and tempo

The neglect of these "intelligent services" reduces the performance in the professional life and blocks the available resources.

The neglect of these "intelligent achievements" in private life and personal relationships creates misunderstandings, tensions, failures and alienation.

The neglect of these "intelligent achievements" generally reduces the potential of self-management and "I"-strength.

Notes and perspectives

How does man (on average) experience his intelligent capabilities?

Write down the key words in this subchapter:

What collectively causes a general lack of interest in learning through reading?

Reading non-fiction regularly is essential because: ...

What did you learn about the value of cognitive learning in the home, school, and church?

What meaning- when living together- has the conversation about the use of words?

Which learning interest predominates in politics and economy?

What does advertising convey about learning?

Formulate an important question about the outcome when there are differences in thinking:

3.1.3. Thinking and its psychological feedback

"Permanent education" is the guiding idea of adult education. Learning takes an entire lifetime.

A profession requires continuous. The young man emancipates himself from his parents' home, throws his textbooks in a corner and thinks of his past: "Now it is possible to live." The more demanding a career goal and the job, the more self-evident is learned regularly: Languages, technical, business and management, research, and innovation.

One part of the humanity learns little after school, while another part is constantly learning, especially in a job-oriented way. What do people learn about themselves? How do you perceive yourself? How do you think about your thinking? How do you reflect on your speech? How do you experience and analyze the connection of the intelligent functions with their actions?

Two facts are to be looked at:

People do not learn much about the psychic life at home or at school. There appears to be no space in the curriculum that dream interpretation and meditation, the power of love and the unconscious should be consciously and deeply integrated into life design, for a lifetime.

The other fact is: Young people have little opportunity to acquire life skills within the context of school-based education. For example, talking with a partner, having empathy with a partner, sexuality and the power of love, searching for meaning and values from the psychological inner life, responsibility and obligations over self-love and the spirit, shaping of the outer individual and collective living spaces for the human being (with his psyche), and much more!

The integration of the psychological reality into the "I" guidance to thinking processes is a life demand! This we conclude from the harm and suffering that the unconscious way of life causes worldwide.

Learning in this area makes enables to understand one's own destiny and to take it by the hand. Everyone can learn languages. Even technical things are, to a certain extent, neutral in value as an objective learning process.

But learning about psychological life requires honesty, self-love, and humility.

The more a human comprehensively and diversely opens the psychological life in his consciousness and processes it mentally, the more constructive the powers of the psychic organism become in daily actions.

The 'profit' lies in the human quality of life and in the external quality of life. The objective thinking processes become a different basement and a deeper anchorage. The internal potential becomes a constructive life force.

Reflections and Discussion

If a human learns little about his psychological powers, then he has little ability to integrate his psychic life into the "I" leadership.

Thinking about the psychological life requires means to look for it. The perception is predominantly inside oriented. The process includes:

☐ Empathizing yourself
☐ Listen to your inner voice
☐ Imagining
☐ Looking at your dreams
☐ Understanding your emotions
☐ Paying attention to psycho-physical reactions

Favorable dispositions for learning about mental life are:

☐ Openness
☐ Interest
☐ Positive main attitude to the psyche
☐ Willingness for interior orientation
☐ Devotion to values like love
☐ Do not being fixated on the material
☐ Free from dogmatism
☐ Free from ideological "laws"
☐ Curiosity about the inner experience
☐ Patience and perseverance

A human can learn much about his psychical life and use what he has learned in life:

☐ Identifying, considering, and adequately addressing needs
☐ Recognizing, understanding, clarifying emotions, and thus living constructively.
☐ Recognizing and building the power of love in all walks of life

☐ Using the inner spirit in dream and meditation for daily life
☐ Recognizing and using the "I" and its auxiliary functions
☐ Promoting and using the possibilities of intelligent functions
☐ Understanding the connections between psyche and habitat
☐ Understanding and rooting constructively the actions

It is also important to reflect the problematic reality: The human being does little integrate his psychic life into the intelligent processes.

Man recognizes his needs one-sidedly, understands his feelings only vaguely, integrates love without special deep growth, does not know his spirit from dreams, sees little subjectivity of the "I" functions and intelligence functions, hardly acts consciously in relation to his entire psychological life and recognizes the external life only superficially in the context of the psychic organism of the people.

Diagram 3.1.3: Thinking processes and life-feedback

Diagramm OS5-3: Denkprozesse und Lebensrückkoppelung

English Translation: Inner / external reality > Perception > Consciousness > Language > Thinking > Learn-result > New consciousness, new internalized reality, new handling patterns > New inner / external reality

Some views of reality

Certain statements are clear, such as, "This house has 16 windows". Anyone can see, count, and possibly make corrections. It gets a little harder when someone says, "I have a headache." This cannot 'see' another person. It could be that this is a way to prevent doing certain work. If the psychoanalyst says that "this disturbance is caused by a secret instinctual desire," it becomes even more difficult. How can this be 'proven'? If a philosopher thinks that "a sense can be wrung from every suffering", this should give rise to considerable protest. But doubt can be argued as well, if something is true. In a simplistic form we would present a few classic positions for the understanding of 'reality'.

Materialistic reality show:
This position completely returns reality to matter and forces entirely subject to material. Reality is comprehensible to measure and numbers. The soul as a reality is denied. Mental functions are materially. It is meaningless to strive for 'higher' values when there are only material values.

Positivistic reality show:
Positivism demands that science confines itself to perceptible facts and their lawful connections. According to the New Positivism, only that which is 'verifiable' ('falsifiable') is "true", to verifying by sensual experience. Reviews are only expressions of feelings. There is only necessity in the field of logic. Language can show that metaphysical (transcendental, spiritual) statements are meaningless. Only the positive given is recognizable.

Phenomenological concept of reality:
This position deals with the realities in consciousness. For appearances reveal themselves to the human being only in the consciousness. Not the (material) objects per se are considered, but their essence in the inner picture. This in turn is historical and temporal. It is not the real facts that are the subject of scientific reflection, but their 'essence', their meaning.

Psychologism:
The psycho-spiritual reality is of a spiritual nature. Everything given is given as an experience. Mental causes cause the conclusion of a judgment. These are the norm of the truth. Decisive are the thinking functions.

Spiritual Science Reality Show:

It regards the spiritual understanding polar to the scientifically world of nature and its objectifications, e.g. the culture, the religion, the languages. Spiritual life unfolds historically. So, it is primarily about understanding what has been created historically. The orientation is the individual, the specific.

Rationalism:
The rationalism emphasizes the reason. This, in turn, is often contrasted with revelatory belief and irrational soul forces. Reason is the source of knowledge and for claims to cognition. These have priority over sensually mediated experiences. Decisive is therefore 'correct thinking'.

Behaviorism:
This position argues that only objectively measurable and observable behavior can be the subject of science. The description of contents of the consciousness should be completely dispensed. Thinking, feeling, and perceiving are recorded only as physiological (physical) processes.

Ecological facts in the thought processes

We take from the relevant press and literature some facts from the catalog of environmental problems, given in a nutshell. The key question is: How does man process these 'realities'? For this purpose, the student has the opportunity to formulate his own experiences about thinking and managing the processes:

1. Fact: In Spain there are several million unemployed and 12-15 million directly affected (2012).
2. Fact: The gap between poverty and wealth is growing in Europe.
3. Fact: Psychic suffering has reached "mega dimensions" in Europe.
4. Fact: Millions of people suffer from loneliness, meaninglessness, despair, and fears.
5. Fact: The environmental damage is huge and lead to unimagined long-term effects.

Perception: Do you perceive these facts to be true?	
Awareness: What kind of consciousness do you have regarding these facts?	
Language: How do you summarize these Facts?	
Thinking: What do you think about these facts? How do you judge these facts?	
Learning outcome: What new have you learnt latterly?	
New consciousness: How changed your consciousness through learning?	
Action: How will you newly act these facts with your new level of awareness?	
New external reality: In which way will change your external reality through your actions?	

Recommendation:
Gather information about these facts. Answer the questions:

Notes and Perspectives

How does man (on average) experience the repercussions of his thinking?

Write down the key words in this subchapter:

What do defective thinking processes about mental life cause?

Reflecting on favorable dispositions for learning is essential because:

What did you learn about concepts of reality in your parents' home, school, and church?

What significance in living together has the conversation about thinking and life?

Which ecological facts are not well thought through in politics and the economy?

What does advertising communicate about ecological facts?

Formulate an important question for the perception of mental life:

3.1.4. Exercises

1. When you look at the world or watch TV, do other people see how you consciously reflect and control your perception?

2. How differentiated and according to which quality aspects do you perceive the closer and the further personal living environment?

3. When you think and talk, how do you deal with the variety of meaning of many words?

4. When you read something, listen to someone, or watch TV, how do you interpret the "messages" given?

5. How do you think about your thinking and what does your thinking ability mean to you?

6. How do you feel about your inner psychic life and about your outer life?

7. How do you experience your intellectual learning (increase, stagnation, difficulties, joy)?

8. In what ways do you seek new (advanced) answers and solutions to life questions?

9.a) Assess your perception:

☐ Superficially or profound
☐ Vaguely or clear
☐ Myopic or sighted
☐ Dull or awake
☐ Stained or factual

Comment:

9.b) Assess your thinking:

☐ Prejudiced or prejudice
☐ Superficially or profound
☐ Mingling or differentiated
☐ Fixed or creative
☐ Confused or clear

Comment:

9.c) Assess your language usage:

☐ Diffuse or clear
☐ Ambiguous or clear
☐ Emotively judgmental or factual
☐ Stereotyped or selected
☐ Undifferentiated or differentiated

Comment:

9.d) Assess your learning:

☐ Little or a lot
☐ Immobile or innovative
☐ Rigid or prospectively
☐ Aimlessly or targeted
☐ Partially or holistically

Comment:

10. Do you accept "permanent learning" as a vital requirement? Find your learning disabilities and learning difficulties!

Mark what applies to you:

☐ I do not feel like learning new things
☐ I mostly lack the motivation to learn
☐ I learn something new if it is of interest to me
☐ I do not know for what reason I should learn something
☐ I have little desire for discovery and little curiosity
☐ I am intellectually unresponsive
☐ When I learn, it should be concrete and exciting
☐ I doubt if much learning still makes sense today

☐ My interest is mostly short-lived and quickly gone
☐ I am somehow blocked to learning something new
☐ I have little confidence in my learning ability
☐ I have little faith in my judgment
☐ Effort and discipline are a problem for me
☐ I am afraid to form my own opinions and theoretical hypotheses
☐ I have little experience when taking responsibility for learning
☐ I usually experience stress in learning
☐ It is hard for me to focus on learning
☐ I have no stamina in abstract thinking
☐ I cannot bear contradictions
☐ I am too loaded with problems and conflicts
☐ Stressful experiences from my own school time block me to learn
☐ I cannot accept my lack of knowledge and ability
☐ I do not see the need for lifelong learning
☐ I have a low frustration tolerance
☐ I have never been led to the world of non-fiction
☐ I believe that learning is only for "intellectuals"
☐ I am too much of a consumer to learn to work harder
☐ I have no patience in the struggle for understanding and language
☐ I am internally hampered by dissatisfaction and aversion
☐ I often feel a constant retention of my life force
☐ I have no planned breaks and variety
☐ I am undecided in my own goals and without determination
☐ For all new things, I always want to know first whether it really benefits me
☐ I lack the empathy for different language forms of texts
☐ I do not take the meaning of knowledge / life knowledge to seriously
☐ I am not very willing to learn new things about different subject areas

Number of crosses:

How do you assess and explain your situation?

And now as a conclusion give "the good intentions":

Multiple Choice Test

Select the four correct answers:

5.1. Intelligence functions as a complex system. The intelligent main functions are:

- ☐ a) Thinking
- ☐ b) Perception
- ☐ c) Language / Speech
- ☐ d) Wisdom
- ☐ e) Cognitive learning
- ☐ f) Intuitive ideas

5.2. Quality and performance differences. Central statements are:

- ☐ a) Perception has different qualities
- ☐ b) Physical (material) conditions perceive people the same way
- ☐ c) Language has different subjective aspects
- ☐ d) Thinking operations works by itself
- ☐ e) If two people use the same words, it can still mean something different.
- ☐ f) Cognitive learning presumes interest, willingness, and aware targeted action, separated from exceptions.

5.3. The thinking and its psychological feedback. Favorable dispositions for cognitive learning are:

- ☐ a) Openness to values
- ☐ b) Interest
- ☐ c) Integrity
- ☐ d) Free from ideological thinking
- ☐ e) Suffering
- ☐ f) Internal orientation

3.2. Networked intelligence

3.2.1. The perception and its subjectivity

The reality for man is the result of his perception. Here we focus on the visual perception.

Much of this also applies to listening, smelling, feeling and inner perception. Dreams, imaginations, and intuition are inner perception.

All forms of perception have different qualities and variations in quantity: much-less, differentiated-undifferentiated, complex-simple, strong-weak, and a relative temporal / spatial reference.

Thus, people have different benefits of perceptions, and their internalized reality is also different.

Several men see the same reality mostly different. One only sees rough outlines, another the wholeness and its parts. A third experiences the supplementary sensory perceptions clearly and intensively, while another reacts indistinctly to sound, fragrance, and movement / touch.

The perception is subject to the defense and integration mechanism. The projection plays a particularly important role here: The unconscious influences what a person sees and how he experiences or interprets it.

Feelings, expectations, wishes, and previous experiences determine the performance of the perception.

Habits also control perception. In many cases, perception is an experience at the same time.

Emotions are activated while the perceived is interpreted in terms of sense, meaning and value. Such processes often run fast and "pre-consciously".

Different realities can only be opened with inner perception: The psychological life and the transcendence. Here the interpretation plays a fundamental role.

Reality is then the interpreted experience. Overall, perception is a multifaceted subjective process. The more complex a reality, the more different it is perceived and becomes a differing 'reality' in consciousness.

Reflections and Discussion

The qualities of perception are:

Much-less	Precise-vague	Holistic-incomplete
Differentiated-undifferentiated	one sided-versatile	Profound-superficial

Perception always includes:

☐ A space and time perspective
☐ An interpretation of meaning and meaning
☐ A valuable experience
☐ A bond to already which is an internalized pattern about the realities
☐ Own 'theories' about the realities
☐ Projections, if not dismantled

Perception is part of the intelligent process:

☐ With the perception, a linguistic transformation takes place
☐ Linguistic transformation depends on vocabulary and thought processes
☐ The ability to construct inner images is subject to learning processes

Perception: Reflect on how you perceive other people in general and discuss the consequences of this in a small circle:

How to critically reflect your own / foreign perception:

Vague, diffuse, foggy	Clear, precise, alert
Undifferentiated	Differentiated
Ostensible, superficial	Deep, profound
One-sided, partially	Versatile, comprising
In confusion	In clear order
Coarse-meshed, all in	Fine-grained
Rigid, fixed	Flexible, agile
Nearsighted	Farsighted
Emotional	Factual
Imprudent	Considerate
Indifferent	Responsibly
With diffuse value experience	With clear value experience
Habitually	Willfully, intentionally
With presumptions	With competence

Defensive, absorbing	Integrating
In the narrow ego area	In the extended area of expertise
Concealing, disguising	Revealing
With prejudice	Free from prejudice
Without time perspective	With time perspective
Mingling	Decomposing

Discuss in the group about "subjective perception":

Diagram 3.2.1: The perceptions of the human

1. Space-distance-experience: Residential area, quarters, region, province, nation, continent, earth, cosmos

2. Determine the future: Hour, day, week, month, year, years, 10 years, 25 years, 50 – 100 years

3. Register the past: Hour, day, week, month, year, years, 10 years, 25 years, 50 – 100 years

4. Aspects of differentiations: Vague surface, rough ensemble / outlines of the surface / complexity of cause, effect / microscopical, minute unities

5. Private experience space: Own reality of daily life, social environment / wide public / cooperating tradition – culture – religion – life / networking earth and humanity

6. External & inner realities: External appearances (cover, shell, mask, façade) in cumulative amount / inner perception of the psychological life with cumulative depth and precision

7. Determine of values: Own values / values of others / material assets, values of goods / values of environment & nature / values of the psychic-spiritual

8. Flexibility: The own experiencing / Zeitgeist in the habitat / historical bond tradition – culture / bond to transcendence

3.2.2. Words, their meanings and associations

The everyday language is essentially vague, ambiguous, and inaccurate. Many terms used can have different meanings without a clarified framework. Some words are objective, emotional, judgmental, and interpretive at the same time.

As a result, many people speak the same words but mean different things. They contain a reality in the consciousness in different words. The same words can also trigger different emotions in different people.

Often a word is an individual "theory" and variable emotional experiences for the same person, depending on context and moment. Words often contain different types of statements: factual information, value in judgment, explanation, instruction, desire, command, threat and so on.

A small part of language refers to the concrete empirical reality. A much larger part captures an experience, a value, an individual meaning.

Behind many a word stands a personal 'theory' originated in a life story context. So, humans have their own associations about almost everything.

The word 'teacher' may be unique to all in the context of elementary school. But there are many different images that are related to one's experiences. When one speaks of 'love', one thinks of parental love, another to his mother, a third to sexuality, a fourth to the outcasts of society. What is pleasant for one person is interpreted by another as 'unpleasant'. Words such as 'trust', 'self-fulfillment', 'happiness', 'success,' 'joy', and many more, trigger with each experiential memory.

Everyone links his own images and interests with such words. What "cooperation" contains, how have to be "nice holidays", which emotions a 'car' triggers depends on the person, not on a dictionary.

The simpler the words, the 'theories' and associations from a human, the simpler is 'his' reality.

Questions and additions:

a) How do you experience the variety of meanings of your personal language?

b) Collect some communication problems based on the subjectivity of language:

Reflections and Discussion

A word or a statement can contain different levels of meaning. For example:

- ☐ Factual information
- ☐ Shared experience
- ☐ Prejudice
- ☐ Factual conclusion
- ☐ Threat
- ☐ Action suggestion

- ☐ A valued judgment
- ☐ Subjective theory
- ☐ Hypothesis
- ☐ Request
- ☐ Forecast
- ☐ Declaration

The way someone uses his language is also an expression of his world relationship:

- ☐ Hurtful and offensive
- ☐ Reflective
- ☐ Experience-based
- ☐ Vulgar
- ☐ Threatening or punishing

- ☐ Devaluing and worthless
- ☐ Exaggerating
- ☐ Emotional
- ☐ Emphasizes polite
- ☐ Disinterested and boring

The associations to words are an important part of the recording of the reality:

- ☐ Life experiences
- ☐ Zeitgeist
- ☐ Anxiety occupation

- ☐ Property assignment
- ☐ Linked need
- ☐ Triggering hope

In a group, discuss the details of each to the following scheme:

Words	Meaning	Feelings	Associations
Judge			
Priest			
Love			
Sympathy			
Sex			
Dishonest			
Party			
Tram			
Luck			

Interpret in the group which communication problems arise from these.

Diagram 3.2.2: The relation reality-language-consciousness

Diagramm OS5-5: Das Verhältnis Wirklichkeit-Sprache-Bewusstsein

Wirklichkeiten:

Eigene psychische
Wirklichkeit

Lebensraum mit den
Dingen/Gegebenheiten

Andere Menschen
mit ihrer Psyche

Transzendente Welt
Göttliches/Philosophie

Sprache:

Sachlich	Vorurteil
wertend	gebunden an Lehren
emotional	Assoziationen
erklärend	Lebensgeschichte
interpretierend	zukunftsbezogen
auffordernd	handlungsbezogen
logisch	theoriebezogen

Im Bewusstsein:

Die wahrgenommenen Bilder
Veränderungen in den Bildern
Die Anpassung an vorhandene Inhalte
Die sprachliche Konstruktion
Die Verarbeitung mit Sprache

English Translation:
Realities: Own psychological reality / Habitat with things & facts / Other humans with their Psyche / Transcendental world, divine, philosophy >
Language: Factual – prejudice, judgmental – bond in doctrine, emotional – associations, explanatory – Life story, interpreting – future-oriented, calling – actions-oriented, logical – theory-oriented >
In the consciousness: The perceived images, changes in the images, adaption to existing contents, the linguistic construction, the handling with language

3.2.3. The talking and the phrases about the realities

Man absorbs many realities through communication: to the spoken and written word, partly with and partly without images, partly close to the image, partly far from pictorial reality. The communicated reality has here undergone a special process by the mediating person or by a medium (radio, television, newspaper, book).

Human aspects shape the information about realities. There are many factors at work. We can identify these in all psychological subsystems. Let us emphasize here some special factors: The communication depends on the relationship between those persons. If a human speaks to another or to a group, then the emotional factors are considerably influencing.

Important are fear of rejection or criticism, self-centeredness, sympathy and anti-sympathy, the already familiar language code (in both parts) and much more. Furthermore, here are often own interests in the game. Through communication, humans often want to achieve something, be it in prestige, a factual advantage, power, or a purposeful influence in the direction of a plot impulse.

We know the manipulation of reality with the language of politics, advertising, and press messages. People are inclined to accept the realities as they are linguistically and, at best, coupled with images.

For the expression of language, people practice other forms of shaping that help shape the communicated reality. The nonverbal communication is an important aspect. With mimicry, gestures, emphasis, and certain movements (e.g. scratching, looking away) the communicated content is accentuated. In the case in the recipient, mental factors further change the way they are received, whether through selection or interpretation. People with feelings of anxiety, with inferiority, with special vulnerability or a strong emotional need for protection see and hear under these factors.

The external presentation of a message about a reality also takes place under external circumstances, such as clothes, rank of the person, meaning of the person, for the receiver. It should be noted only in passing that information about a reality can also be intentionally distorted.

Reflections and Discussion

Human aspects in conversation are:

Personal language	Inferiority feelings
Emotional reference to words	Fears
Covert Interests	"I" relatedness
Intentions of actions	Role expectations / orientation

Types of speech form the message content:

Friendly	Cordial	Humiliating	Devaluating
Aggressively	Sentencing	Hostile	Encouraging
Bored	Emotional		

The message about a reality is co-formed by secondary factors:

Tone	Subplots	Habitat elements
Gestures	Facial expression	Moment

Imagine: A person tells you about an event. Thereby you recognize different nonverbal elements.

How do these affect the content? Discuss such experiences in a group.

Nonverbal elements	Meaning for the genuine message
To look hard in the e	
Scratching yourself while talking	
Strict look	
Gesticulating	
Touching the receiver	
Taking a deep breath	
Adjusting clothes	
Sighing or coughing	
Looking at the clock	

What nonverbal patterns do others recognize about you? Ask others!

Diagram 3.2.3: The intermediation of messages with language

Diagramm OS5-6: Die Vermittlung von Botschaften mit Sprache

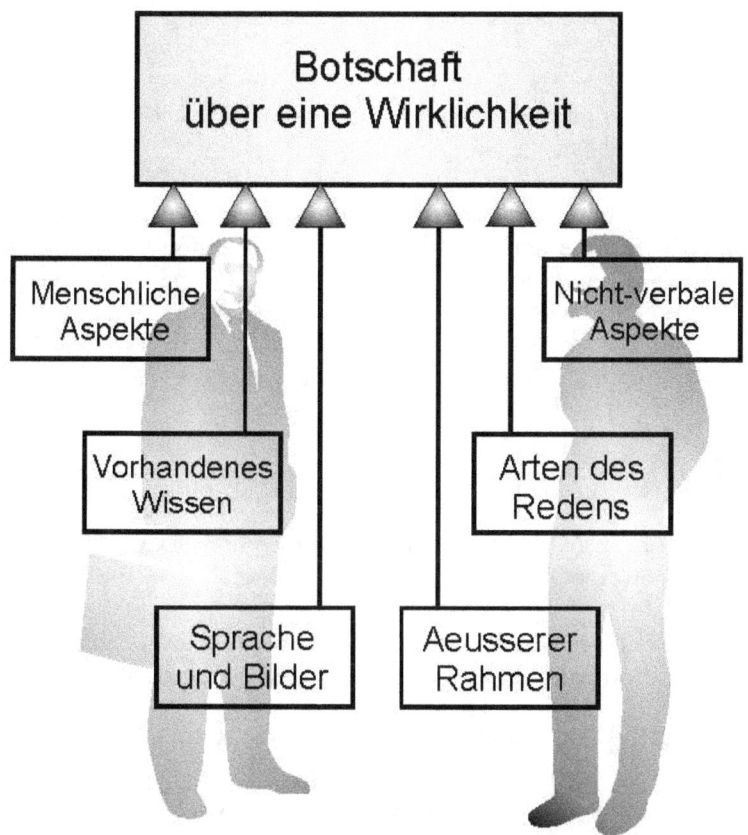

English Translation: Human aspects & available knowledge & language and images & external frame & kind of talking & nonverbal aspects influence **Message over a reality**

3.2.4. Thinking and the intelligent operations

Thinking is a working process. The first step is the linguistic comprehension of the recorded inner and / or outer reality. This is about choosing the right words.

Thinking operations are possible. The linguistically perceived is incorporated into the already existing realities in the memory.

Some adaptation, e.g. transformation of the reality is possible. In this assignment, the reality is subdivided and assigned categories: The same to the same and the like to the like.

In addition is to compare, combinate, interpret and associate. Logical operations become important here. Structuring processes are the search for functional relationships, the determination of cause and effect, the connection with action goals and the construction of the parts into a whole.

Thinking about the future can be constructed for a reality: "If this continues, then ...".

In all these processes, existing knowledge plays a significant role.

It can also be assumed that in addition to the purely linguistic processing also a pictorial, an emotional and a valuing take place.

These "works" are based entirely on the existing life experience, including the knowledge learned. These thinking processes also involve creative forces, with the search for new classes and structures, for new combinations and for not yet recognized extensions in the linguistic-pictorial processing.

Of special importance is the ability to process perceptions of psychic realities.

In many cases, people are only inaccurately differentiated from foreign psychic realities and experience much of the world self-involved.

The practical life use of the conceptually processed reality is another aspect of intelligent abilities. The more complex and difficult it is to grasp the reality, the more the "I" is required to form and use the thinking.

Reflections and Discussion

Thinking operations are:

☐ Forming concepts
☐ Finding words
☐ Capturing meaning
☐ Assigning values
☐ Abstracting of space / time
☐ Managing flexibility
☐ Identifying feelings
☐ Using knowledge
☐ Using intuition
☐ Capturing relations
☐ Forecasting
☐ Creating categories
☐ Purposeful processing
☐ Evaluating action-oriented
☐ Logical reasoning
☐ Integrating of new
☐ Storing

There are various psychical forces in thought processes. These include:

☐ Feelings
☐ Psychodynamics
☐ Meditations
☐ Needs
☐ Unconscious inventory
☐ Actions
☐ Dreams
☐ Ability to love

Thinking performance aspects can be captured as follows:

Performance aspect:	Areas of life:
☐ Rich vocabulary	
☐ Fresh memory	
☐ Purposeful thinking	
☐ Good memory	
☐ Logical thinking	
☐ Skilled in language	
☐ Disassemble complex	

☐ Mobile in detecting something new	
☐ Recognize relations	
☐ Structuring ability	
☐ Using of intuition	
☐ Integrating of spontaneous ideas	
☐ Thinking the unimaginable	
☐ Capturing difficulties linguistically	
☐ Flexible thinking patterns	
☐ Flexible in an emotional experience	
☐ Open in a valuing experience	

How do people see the achievements thinking of others?

Diagram 3.2.4: Reception and processing of realities

Diagramm OS5-7: Aufnahme und Verarbeitung von Wirklichkeiten

Innere Wirklichkeiten
Aeussere Wirklichkeiten

Faktoren der Aufnahme und Verarbeitung der Wirklichkeit:

Wahrnehmungsfähigkeit	Assoziative Verknüpfung
Erleben	Komplexe
Emotionale Auslösung	Projektionen
Erkenntnisinteresse	Identifikationen
Kommunikationsinteresse	Abwehrmechanismen
Normen, Werte	Realitätsinteresse
Selektionsmechanismen	Offenheit für Neues
Gefühle	Lernbereitschaft
Bedürfnisse	Indizieninterpretation
Denken	Raum-/Zeiterleben
Persönliche Interessen	Unerkannte Reizaufnahmen
Vorstellungsmuster	Ueberzeugungen
Ideale	Selbstbestätigungstendenz
Leiden	Sprachliche Fähigkeiten
Psychischer Zustand	Wortschatz/Ausdruck

English Translation: Inner realities & external realities take effect to factors of the reception and processing of the reality: Perceptual ability – associative combination, experiencing – complexes, emotional activating – projections, interest of knowledge – identifications, interest of communication – defense mechanism, norms & values – interest of reality, selectivity mechanism – openness for the new, feelings – willingness to learn, needs – interpretation of sings, thinking – experiencing of space & time, personal interests – undetected reception of stimulus, ideational patterns – convictions, ideals – tendency of self-affirmation, suffering – linguistical abilities, psychological situation – vocabulary & expression

3.2.5. The judgments (values) and the prejudices

Man perceives realities valuing. He experiences these as pleasant or unpleasant, sensible or meaningless, good or evil, and thus as a value. As the human experiences a lot emotionally, so this reality includes also a meaning.

There is no "value-free reality" for man. But people can experience different values for the same realities. In addition to these experienced valuing man can form "value judgments" for all realities. That is, he makes linguistically well-formulated statements that he validates in some way: "This is good (or bad), because ...".

Many words contain value elements, such as: sympathetic or unsympathetic, right or wrong, honest or dishonest, beautiful or ugly, useful or useless, harmonic or disharmonious, and many more. 'Humanism', 'freedom', 'justice', 'self-determination' and 'emancipation' are all values, i.e. certain people have determined that these values should be promoted and lived as positive.

Ethical and moral judgments are causally related to an action, by which is given with a promise or rejection and a nominal demand. For example, "That is good and therefore allowed ..." or, "That's bad and therefore reprehensible ...". People do not always recognize this, and therefore, have attitude pattern that are just positive or negative.

If these judgments are built into a linguistic system and substantiated in some way, then one speaks of 'beliefs'. For some, these systems are 'utilitarian' -, e.g. arguing the usefulness. For others these systems are 'religious', e.g. established in the context of religious or philosophical teachings. Therefore, these systems are based on constructed ideas about man and life, e.g. hedonic or metaphysical (spiritual).

The justification of values can also be based directly on the reality: Man needs education; therefore, he should develop himself.

Prejudices are judgments valuating the elements of reality after a certain pattern without thinking and without justification.

Reflections and Discussion

Many words contain value elements:

Beautiful /ugly	Good / bad
Sympathetic/unsympathetic	Tidy /messy
Disciplined / undisciplined	Interesting / boring
Cared / neglected	Free / unfree
Moderated /excessive	Tolerant / intolerant
Honest / dishonest	Selfish / selfless

Value judgments directly or indirectly contain a TARGET claim:

☐ To be helpful to old people
☐ To tell the truth and not to lie
☐ To respect foreign ownership
☐ People should love and not hate
☐ To conform to sexuality ideals
☐ To not exploit other people
☐ To not humiliate, hurt, or torture other people
☐ To protect nature
☐ To not kill
☐ To not eat meat
☐ To go to church on Sunday

Prejudices are for examples :

☐ Strangers are mostly dangerous people
☐ The X-humans are stupid
☐ The Y people are working shy
☐ The Z-humans are devious
☐ Decent people are good people
☐ The world is alright
☐ My religion is the true religion.

Many values are ideologically or religiously founded, regardless of the wholeness of the psychic organism.

Discuss values and judgments based on the psychic organism in a small circle.

Diagram 3.2.5: The aspects of value justifying

Diagramm OS5-8: Die Aspekte der Wertbegründungen

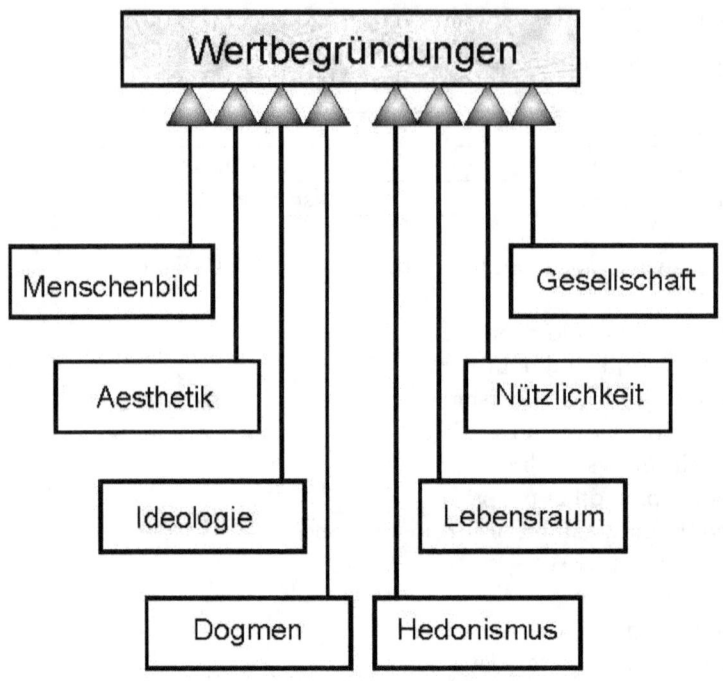

These 1: Der Mensch übernimmt durch Erziehung,
Sozialisation und Enkulturation die Werte und
Soll-Urteile seines Umfeldes.

These 2: Wertbegründungen basieren auf realem
Wissen (Erkenntnissen) oder auf eingebildetem
Wissen und verlangen immer einen Willensakt.

English Translation: Value justifying is influenced by idea of man &
esthetic & ideology & dogmas & hedonism & habitat & usefulness & society
Thesis 1: The human adopts trough education, socialization and
enculturation the values and target judgements of his environment.
Thesis 2: Value justifying bases upon real knowledge (findings) or imaginary
knowledge and demand always an act of volition.

3.2.6. The thinking learning in life

The intelligent functions, from perception to value judgments, are formed through education and then through the life. Everyone has the opportunity to further differentiate these learned skills. The use of these psychological functions presupposes an act of will and a conscious "I" guidance of the operations.

If one looks at people's lives and the effects, one must conclude that people think little and often inaccurately. This evolves a circular conclusion: The result is the activating basis for the intellectual learning. If man designs his life with little thinking effort, then the result is the condition for possible learning processes.

The processed reality has in acting the actual reference back to life. Thus, the cycle is closed hence reception of reality. The psychological functions contain great opportunities for everybody.

Because thinking is an active achievement, it requires concentration, affection, will, discipline, self-control, interest, and some more activities. The elementary requirement is the need for learning. Many people organize learning in the field of professional development or leisure activities (music, art, sports, languages).

Few are familiar with the fact that there are many things to learn about the psychological subsystems. The problems of industrialized society (as well as other societies) give rise to the assumption that people learn little about the effects of their actions.

Rigid attitudes, attachment to 'artificial' needs, and blockage in emotions, hamper the entry into thinking learning. Learning requires a certain willingness to take risks, to have curiosity or the will to discover, to have love for life, readiness for self-reflection, and a awareness of responsibility about oneself and the prospective effects of one's own life.

Learning for a lifetime is a life-long commitment, says adult education. Learning does not have to stop when you graduate, even not at mid-life or retirement age. Older people can learn as much as young people. Without learning, the mental-spiritual evolution is not realizable: There is no argument that says that the retired person can no longer learn or has nothing to learn.

Reflections and Discussion

Learning to think requires some prerequisites:

- ☐ Concentration
- ☐ Will
- ☐ Curiosity
- ☐ "I" guidance
- ☐ Working framework
- ☐ Learning needs
- ☐ Planning
- ☐ Motivation
- ☐ Openness
- ☐ Stimulation readiness

Creativity in thinking is based on:

- ☐ Independence of foreign judgments
- ☐ Internal flexibility
- ☐ Free of fixed ideas
- ☐ Willingness to make mistakes
- ☐ Sense for new ways of thinking
- ☐ Being free from white-black thinking
- ☐ Openness to interior experiences
- ☐ Strong attachment to life
- ☐ Interest in the power of the spirit
- ☐ Freedom in the material
- ☐ Determination for tasks
- ☐ To be free from dogmatic teachings

Psychological learning conditions that can be learned / educated, vary often for different life situations.

Learning conditions:	Concrete situation:
Flexible attitudes	
Achievement interest	
Open-minded attitude	
Flexibility in role behavior	
Desire to create / design joy	
Willingness to be challenged	
Personal growth interest	
Accepting your own weaknesses	
Enthusiasm	

Free from stereotyping	
Assessment before value judgment	
Respect for people, nature, goods	
Self-confidence	
Realistic ideals	
Personal responsibility	
Endurance	
Accepting the non-knowledge	

Group discussion: Learning requirements for people in general.

Diagram 3.2.6: Learning ability for the life coping

Diagramm OS5-9: Lernfähigkeit zur Lebensbewältigung

English Translation: Thinking ability, perceptions, memory & will, willing, interest, decisions & guidance, concentration, control & life attention, life attitudes, life experiences influence the **Learning ability for the life coping.**

3.2.7. Working unit

3.2.7. Working unit - 1

1. a) How do you experience your perception?

1. b) Extend the problem of subjectivity of perception with your own experiences:

2. a) Perception: Reflect on how you generally perceive other people and interpret the consequences. Mark what applies to you:

6 = complete; 5 = very; 4 = predominantly; 3 = medium; 2 = partial; 1 = little; 0 = not

Vague, diffuse, foggy	Clear, precise, alert
Undifferentiated	Differentiated
Ostensible, superficial	Deep, profound
One-sided, partially	Versatile, inclusive
In confusion	In clear order
Coarse-meshed, all in	Fine-grained
Rigid, fixed	Flexible, mobile
Nearsighted	Farsighted
Emotional	Factual
Imprudent	Considered
Indifferent	Responsible
With ambiguous value experience	With clear value experience
Habitual	Deliberately, intentional
With presumptions	With competence
Defensive, absorbing	Receiving, integrating
In the narrow ego area	In the extended area of expertise
Concealing, disguising	Revealing
With prejudice	Free from prejudice
Without time perspective	With time perspective
Mingling	Decomposing

Total score: ....   Total score: ....

2. b) What is your interpretation?

3. Formulate an educational goal for your perception:

4. a) Imagine your perception:

4. b) Your conclusion in one sentence:

3.2.7. Working unit - 2

1. a) For your personal language, how do you experience the variety of meanings?

1. b) Describe a communication problem arising from the subjectivity of the language:

2. a) Give to the words your meaning, your feeling, and your associations:

Words	Meaning	Feelings	Associations
Judge			
Priest			
Love			
Sympathy			
Sex			
Dishonest			
Party			
Tram			
Luck			

2. b) Interpret what communication problems arise from this interpretations:

3. Formulate an educational goal for your personal use:

4. a) Imagine your language characteristics, what are they?

4. b) Your conclusion in one sentence:

3.2.7. Working unit - 3

1. a) How do you experience the communication of realities by the media?

1. b) Extend the human aspects of designing information:

2. a) Imagine that a person tells you about an event. Thereby you recognize different nonverbal elements. How do these affect the content?

The event in key words:

Nonverbal elements	Meaning of for the actual message
To look hard in the eyes	
Scratching yourself while talking	
Strict look	
Gesticulating	
Touching the receiver	
Taking a deep breath	
Adjusting clothes	
Sighing or coughing	
Looking at the clock	

2. b) Which nonverbal patterns do you recognize in yourself?

3. Formulate an educational goal in terms of "message delivery":

4. a) Imagine about your non-verbal language:

4. b) Your conclusion in one sentence:

3.2.7. Working unit - 4

1. a) How do you experience your intellectual processing of recorded realities?

1. b) How do people generally work on their recorded realities?

2. a) Thinking performance aspects can be recorded as follows. Tick what's right for you. Keep track of the areas in which you are repeatedly experiencing your particularly favorable performance aspects:

6 = complete; 5 = very; 4 = predominantly; 3 = medium; 2 = partial; 1 = little; 0 = not

Performance aspect:	Life area
☐ Rich vocabulary	
☐ Fresh memory	
☐ Purposeful thinking	
☐ Good memory	
☐ Logical thinking	
☐ Clever in language	
☐ Disassemble complex	
☐ Mobile in detecting something new	
☐ Recognizing relations	
☐ Structuring ability	
☐ Use of intuition	
☐ Integrating spontaneous ideas	
☐ Thinking through the unimaginable	
☐ Capturing difficulties linguistically	
☐ Flexible thinking patterns	
☐ Flexible in the emotional experience	
☐ Open in judgmental experience	

2. b) Total score: ..... Interpret:

3. Formulate an educational goal about your thinking performance aspects:

4. a) Think about your way of thinking:

4. b) Your conclusion in one sentence:

3.2.7. Working unit - 5

1. a) How do you experience the judgmental statements of other people?

1. b) Expand the possibilities of value justification:

2. Give below 2 examples:
2. a) Words with value elements / value aspects are:

2. b) Value judgments with a direct / indirect TARGET claim are:

2. c) Prejudices are:

2. d) A value based on the psychic organism is:

2. e) A judgment based on the psychic organism is:

3. Formulate an educational goal about your judgments:

4. a) Consider how you can develop your values:

4. b) Your conclusion in one sentence:

3.2.7. Working unit - 6

1. a) How do you experience people's willingness to learn?

1. b) Explain what is meant by "learning for a lifetime". Provide your own experiences:

2. Give an example- of where you will experience repeated positive learning conditions for each of the statements listed below:

Learning conditions:	Concrete situation:
Flexible attitudes	
Achievement interest	
Open-minded attitude	
Flexibility in role behavior	
Desire to create / design joy	
Willingness to be challenged	
Personal growth interest	
Accepting your own weaknesses	
Enthusiasm	
Free from stereotyping	
Assessment before value judgment	
Respect for people, nature, goods	
Self-confidence	
Realistic ideals	
Personal responsibility	
Endurance	
Accepting the non-knowledge	

3. Formulate an educational goal regarding learning conditions:

4. a) Consider your willingness to learn:

4. b) Your conclusion in one sentence:

3.2.7. Working unit - 7

As your interlocutor tells you: "There is a lot of exaggeration with 'learning for a lifetime'. This is certainly not that important ... ". Formulate 10 counter arguments:

Multiple Choice Test

Select the four correct answers:

6.1. <u>Perception contains (mostly):</u>
☐ a) The space / time perspective   ☐ b) A valuable experience
☐ c) Nominal judgment   ☐ d) Projection
☐ e) Immediate interpretation   ☐ f) hereditary physiological differences

6.2. <u>The following rates apply:</u>
☐ a) The way someone speaks is an expression of his world relationship.
☐ b) Many words have very different meanings.
☐ c) Associations with spoken words are immaterial background.
☐ d) Reality and language are not the same.
☐ e) Simple situations are taken by all people in approximately the same words.
☐ f) Much of the talking is actually "picture messages".

6.3. <u>Psychic aspects are shown in:</u>
☐ a) Language structure   ☐ b) Facial expressions and gestures
☐ c) Emotional tone   ☐ d) Dialect
☐ e) Experience-related associations   ☐ f) Tone / Volume

6.4. <u>Thinking operations are:</u>
☐ a) Logical thinking   ☐ b) Recognizing relationships
☐ c) Assignment of values   ☐ d) Psycho-energetic forces
☐ e) Abstract   ☐ f) Judging from principles

6.5. The following statements are correct:
☐ a) Value judgments usually have a sentimental reason.
☐ b) Judging is done consciously and thoughtfully throughout.
☐ c) Value judgments directly or indirectly contain a debit claim.
☐ d) Prejudices contain judgmental elements.
☐ e) Settings are emotional value judgments with a visual aspect.
☐ f) Beliefs are logical implications of facts.

6.6. Psychic learning conditions that are learned are:
☐ a) Open-mindedness   ☐ b) Flexible settings
☐ c) Gifts   ☐ d) Differentiated self-image
☐ e) Intelligence services   ☐ f) Driving forces

4. Emotions (Feelings)

Essential theses

The spectrum of feelings of pleasure-displeasure, joy-pain, happiness-unhappiness, and love-hatred are very varied.

Feelings are an expression of the experience, of values, and of meaning.

Feelings can be experienced close to the body (physical feeling) or mentally (sense of value).

Man experiences many overlain and mutual dependent feelings with different quality, quantity, depth, and duration.

Everything that comes into consciousness, from the outside and from within, can trigger emotions. There are many causes. Even the unconscious can create feelings. Feelings can also be created artificially.

Feelings are always the experience of shaped psychological energy. The experience, however, can be disfigured, suppressed or "heated up".

The handling of emotions can be learned. Positive feelings can be built up and shaped resilient.

4.1. Feelings and its Causes

4.1.1. The spectrum of feelings

Daily we all experience feelings: The man, the woman, the child, the employee, the worker, the teacher, the policeman, the doctor, the politician, the parish priest, the director and so on. Whether a person is politically more 'left' or more 'right', Christian, Jew or Muslim, thinking pertinent or fundamental, atheist or archaic-mythological interpreting the existence, he always has feelings.

Emotions play a big role in life. This begins with getting up and becomes particularly clear when if someone has "climbed out of bed with his left leg". Anyone who commutes to work, by public transport, sees the moods of the people, visible on their faces. For some, the mood is gradually changing, increasingly positive or negative at the workplace.

Many are "thawing out" gradually, while others are very vocal and cheerful or moody in communicating early on. Every morning the teacher can set which children are in the same mood or always different. The housewife, alone while cleaning and washing, does her work with certain moods. Anyone who must go to the office of the "Boss" early, or who discusses his daily work with him, will experience him again and again in emotional variations: "With him today, eating cherries is not very good". Even the supervisor experiences his people again and again in different moods.

Throughout the day, emotions change, depending on environmental impacts and occupations. Anyone who makes up the balance of his feelings in the evening, before falling asleep, will be able to detect variations in his feelings, even with a continued basic mood.

Therefore, everyone experiences themselves and others throughout the day with pleasant and unpleasant feelings. Some emotions stimulate and promotes activities and 'carry' through the daily activities. Unpleasant feelings, on the other hand, require more effort for the activities.

Other people, the work and the environment are perceived differently and experienced according to the basic tenor of the feelings.

Anyone who, throughout the course of the day, occasionally focuses on his feelings, will sees themselves in a variety of experiences: "Life is beautiful", "Life is a plague", or "Life is challenging".
Feelings can challenge:

☐ They have an effect on existence
☐ They are the "music" of everyday existence.
☐ They are a vital force:

Emotions urge actions, 'color' the actions, and provoke others into certain behavior.

Therefore, the feelings are elementary expression of life.

Which fool said that feelings were not important?

Reflections and discussion

The spectrum of emotions is manifold. The emotions can be divided into two main categories:

a) Feelings of life-giving, e.g.: love, joy, happiness, harmony, peace, freedom

b) Feelings of avoiding life, e.g.: hate, anger, fear, frustration, aggression, revenge

Feelings are the experience of shaped psychic energy. Each experience activates and creates psychic energy.

The experience is the know-how of meaning and values. In this sense, feelings are always expressions of meaning and value, experienced in real or imaginative situations.

Imaginative thoughts, like fantasy, are an imaginative reality.

The feelings are something like the "music of the existential life".

The experiencing of emotions can be described variably in the dimension "pleasant-unpleasant".

a) Pleasant feelings (pleasure):	Unpleasant feelings (displeasure):
Well	Bad
Fresh, lively	Tired, slack, sluggish

Solving, liberating, relaxing	Restricting, blocking, cramping
Warm	Cold
Harmonizing	Disrupting
Stable	Unstable
Stimulating	Exhaustive
Fulfilling	In deficit
Attractive	Repulsive

The experience of feelings is the experience of existential moments in the outer and in the inner (imagined or internalized) reality.

There is no one without feelings. But there are people who experience many and others who experience little emotions.

The emotions are formed psychical energy.

This energy is the life force.

Feelings are an expression of life.

Diagram 4.1.1: The spectrum of emotions

Diagramm OS6-1: Das Spektrum der Gefühle

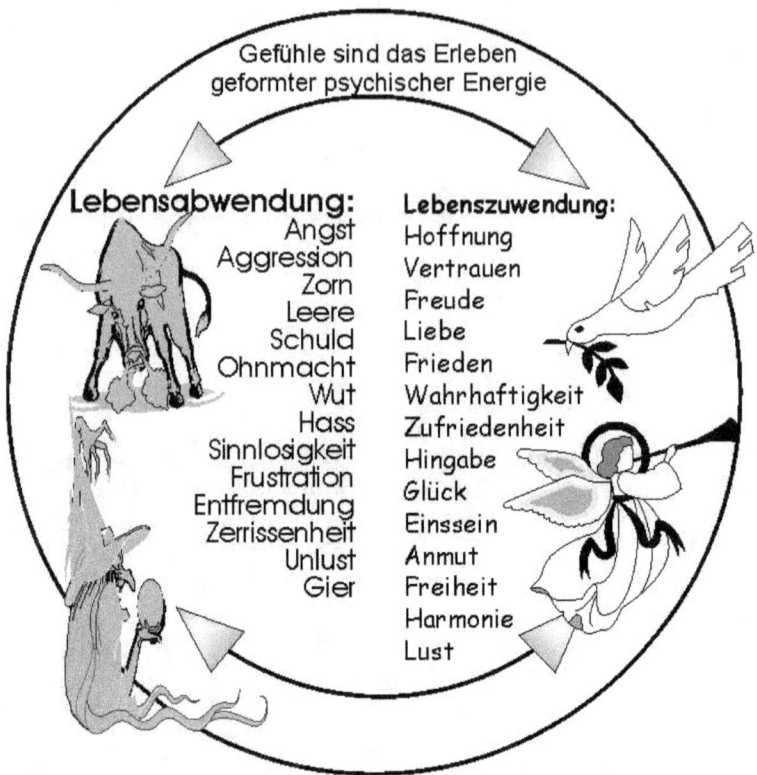

English Translation: Emotions are the experiencing of shaped psychical energy:

Feelings of avoiding life: Fear, aggression, anger, emptiness, guilt, impotence, rage, hate, senselessness, frustration, alienation, disruption, displeasure, greed

Feelings of life-giving: Hope, trust, joy, love, peace, truthfulness, satisfaction, devotion, happiness, being oneself, grace, freedom, harmony, lust

Interest and joy

This section will give an analysis of selected feelings, for the purpose of self-reflection and development, and to give understanding that feelings can be integrated into the ego-guidance.

Interest:

☐ Interest is a fundamental condition and motivational force for the daily functioning of man.
☐ Interest is a positive motivation. Interest is an important motivation in the development of skills, social skills, and intelligence.
☐ Interest is the only motivation that can sustain the daily work in a healthy way.
☐ Interest is indispensable for any creative achievement.
☐ Interest generally gives the individual the experience of a clear claim through the thing.
☐ When the feeling of interest makes use of visual perception, the eyes tend to fix on the object and explore it.
☐ The perception of change and the novelty of a thing activate interest.
☐ You get interest in what is new and different.
☐ One also becomes interested by the idea of possibility.
☐ Daydreaming and fantasizing arouse an interest that often refers to novelty or change, especially to goals.
☐ Interest creates the feeling of being engaged, bound, fascinated and curious.
☐ Interest is a desire to explore, to be engaged, or to expand the self through new information and new experiences.
☐ Interest plays an important role in increasing sexual desire, including maintaining a sexual relationship.

Joy:

☐ Joy is not eating, drinking or mating. It is not the same as a sensation of pleasure. She is not drive lust or sense lust.
☐ Often there is joy when you have achieved or created something personally. Nonetheless, hard work, or even creative effort, does not guarantee joy.
☐ Joy is not the same as fun. Joy can be involved in fun and games, but having fun involves more interest-arousal.
☐ Amusement and entertainment are not synonymous with the experience of joy.

☐ Joy is a feeling of self-confidence and meaningfulness, a feeling of being loved and being lovable.

☐ Joy gives you the sensation of coping with the difficulties and inconveniences of life.

☐ Joy is accompanied by complacency, satisfaction with others and the world.

☐ Joy is characterized by an acceptance of selfhood.

☐ Joy is a by-product of perception, thinking, or acting.

☐ Joy can come from the various stages of creative aspiration, discovery, the completion of a creative process, as well as physical activity (for fitness).

☐ Joy can facilitate bondage, commitment or affection; as well social interaction and social responsiveness.

☐ Joy facilitates daily life and work.

☐ The interaction of joy and interest forms a cornerstone of love and tender relationships.

Sorrow and anger:

An overvaluation of material success and performance hinders the emergence of true joy. Superficiality and an excess of criticism block joy. This is the beginning of sorrow and anger.

Sorrow:

☐ Sorrow and sadness are mostly used as synonyms.

☐ Sorrow is a major emotion in depression, but depression is always a complex pattern of emotions, changes in drive states, and affective-cognitive interactions.

☐ Sorrow occurs because of a continued excessive level of stimulation. The possible sources of stimulation are: pain, cold, noise, heat, bright light, loud speaking, disappointment, failure, loss.

☐ Sorrow is an inevitable part of life.

☐ Sorrow tells itself and others that not everything is all right.

☐ Grief can promote remedial strategies, a kind of negative motivation.

☐ Sorrow promotes cohesion in relationships, in groups and communities.

☐ Those who are lonely, isolated and rejected suffer from grief.

☐ Failure and disappointment about oneself (inadequacies) promotes sorrow.

☐ Experiencing grief is described as sadness, depression, discouragement, loneliness, isolation.

☐ The punishing socialization of grief can cause coercive behavior, low tolerance for frustrations, weak personhood, and loss of physical bravery.

Anger:

- Anger is a fundamental emotion.
- Anger is often accompanied by disgust and contempt.
- A common stimulus for anger is the feeling of being physically or mentally inhibited by something you want to do intensely.
- When something prevents the achievement of a particularly desirable goal or aspect of self-realization, anger almost certainly occurs.
- Low levels of anger can be suppressed for a long time, at the cost of health and at risk of outburst of rage.
- Other causes of anger include: personal insult, everyday frustrations, interruption of interest and joy, to be overreached and compulsion to do something against his will.
- Persistent, unknitted grief triggers anger.
- In anger, the blood boils, the face gets hot and the muscles are tense. One has a sense of power and an impulse to strike the source of anger. So much energy is mobilized that one thinks to burst if you do not bite, hit, or kick your foot.
- In evolution, anger was important to survival. Energies are mobilized to defend oneself.
- The suppression of anger causes psycho-somatic suffering.
- The image of anger includes: Aggression, vengefulness, aggressiveness, being incensed, tension, feelings of injustice, being hurt, grief, hate, dislike, destruction.
- The combination of anger, disgust, or contempt for the sexual drive can lead to deviant, abusive sexual activity.
- Rage can relieve grief or take its place.
- Anger, disgust, and contempt have limiting effects on perception and thinking.

Notes and Perspectives

How does man (on average) handle the spectrum of his feelings?

Write down the key words in this subchapter:

What causes a defective recognition of one's own feelings?

Reflecting on one's own feelings is essential because:

What did you learn in the home, school, and church about the effects and causes of feelings?

What meaning in living together has the conversation about current feelings?

Which feelings predominate in politics and economy?

What does advertising promote for positive and negative feelings?

Formulate an important question for life support:

4.1.2. The characteristics of the emotions

Feelings have some typical characteristics that we all know: A feeling can shape an existing experience over days and weeks.

'Being depressed' means: This feeling depresses and weighs heavily. For example, a person who is in love, full of hope for an expected event or has experienced happiness, will be sustained by such a feeling over a longer period. The opposite applies to the oppressed man.

With music he lives his life forces. Many experiences their work, even their lives, as rather boring. The TV program offers a remedy, at least for the evening: action, excitement, humor, and sex.

This way, you can cover up distressing feelings and fix them for a while. After that, they overcome you again. A tragic family history, social events and even a few small facts from the world, pictorially carried into the living room, often come close to the television consumer.

Many are not able to change their feelings as quickly as the moderator's theme: from an accident or a martial event to sports or the weather. Thus, the spectator is bathed in many different "emotional baths".

The consumer society offers us many opportunities to drown a feeling for minutes.

Casual events can also distract from an emotional mood: an encounter or a telephone call can change one's emotional state.

Man experiences various superimposed feelings daily, one of short, others of longer duration; some profound, others superficial.

But the "play of this music" has even more variations: a feeling can bring about other feelings.

Oppressed feelings are presented in a new form:

☐ Those who are aggressive and depressed may perhaps conceal a deeper grief.
☐ Who is optimistic, may have experienced something pleasant shortly before.

☐ Anyone who experiences powerlessness in terms of environmental pollution may experience a deeper helplessness in his own life.

☐ Those who have been much humbled may express cynical or sadistic feelings. Those who experience feelings of guilt, repress them, and do not take them seriously, e.g. may feel a diffuse fear or an unfathomable oppression.

☐ For some, life seems banal, difficult, or hopeless. The flight into fantasies revives. He internally gains influence in a new mood. He dreams of a beautiful life, of a good relationship, of money and goods.

☐ Inner ideas activate psychic energy and thus feelings.

☐ Feelings are sense and value experiences and evoked from inside or outside.

Reflections and Discussion

Feelings can be perceived from different points of view. Of these, the most important aspects are highlighted here:

- ☐ A feeling can last a long time or be short-lived.
- ☐ A feeling can be profound or superficial.
- ☐ A feeling can be experienced more physically or more mentally.
- ☐ A feeling can be strong / intense or rather weak.

Rarely does a human have only one feeling. In many cases, long-lasting basic feelings are partly superimposed by profoundly shorter and partly superficial and only briefly intensified feelings. It is therefore often difficult to discern which feelings are to be understood as "following feelings" or as "strengthened" feelings. A superimposed emotion can have an effect that does not correspond to the feeling. An energy charge comes from a deeper, covered feeling. Some feelings then cause a changed new emotional state, for example:

- ☐ Frustration causes aggression
- ☐ Fainting leads to fear
- ☐ The feeling of repressed lust leads to guilt
- ☐ Guilt causes anxiety and / or depression

Emotions are, consciously or unconsciously, bound to 'realities'. The external realities (life systems and its elements) are as important as the internal realities (the psychic organism as the "object of consciousness").

Emotionally, people react differently to external and internal realities. This depends, among other things, on the subjective meaning of a reality (or an element of it).

The psychic energy of the emotions forms the psychodynamics, affects the thinking and acting, can influence all psychic forces considerably. The formed psychical energy also has a significant effect on the body.

Diagram 4.1.2: Characteristics and aspects of emotions

Diagramm OS6-2: Charakteristiken und Aspekte der Gefühle

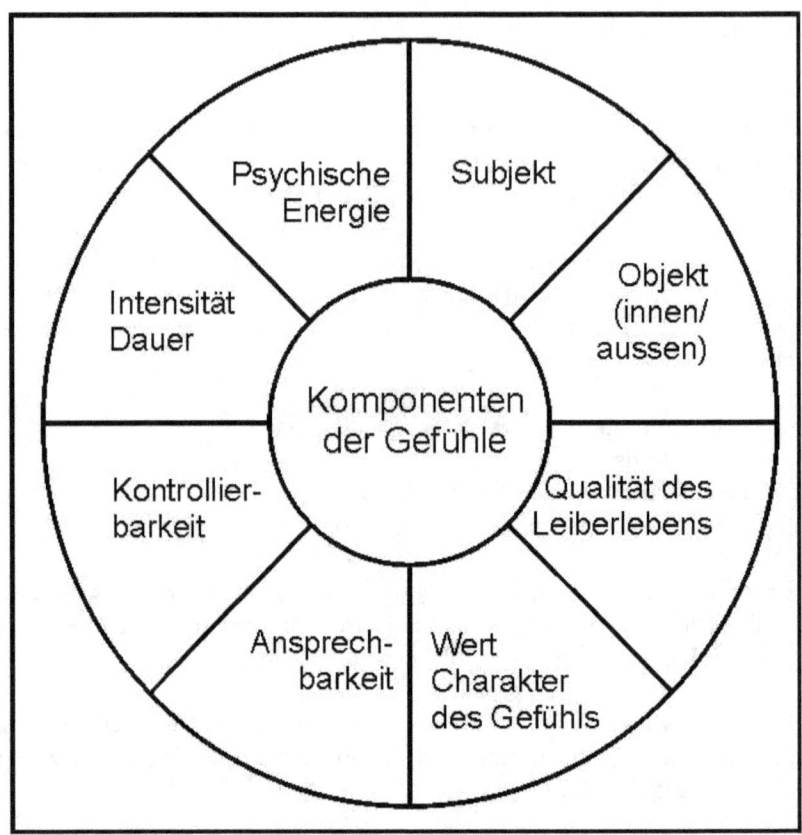

English Translation: Components of emotions: Subject, object (internal / external, quality of experiencing the body, value / character of the emotion, responsiveness, checkability, intensity / durability, psychical energy

The Subjective Emotional Experience

Everyone has his own way of reacting emotionally; and everyone experiences in a very personal way the value of his emotional experience. This value character is an expression of the whole person. It reflects partly attitudes, partly value patterns, partly convictions, partly norms and partly prejudices. This section of the book allows you to systematically get to know aspects of your own person.

Write down in the right column your experience and the value (positive-negative) that you give to each experience.

Picture, emotional Reaction:	Experience:	Value (pos./neg.):
Homeless		
Weeping man		
Fundamentalist		
Determined woman		
A mountain of dishes to clean		
Huge 'living silo'		
Smog		
Drug addict at the train station		
Doctor		
A man with amputated legs		
Dentist's chair		
Strong traffic noise		
Naked woman in the park		
South Sea Islands		
Title page of a porno magazine		
War scene		
Piles of garbage		
A fatal traffic accident		
A hospital operating room		
Images of saints in the church		
Death cell		
Execution chamber USA		
Picture of a happy mother		
A proud father		
A baby on the chest		
Waste on the lake shore		
Polluted rivers / streams		
A strict boss		

Picture, emotional Reaction:	Experience:	Value (pos./neg.):
Dead trees		
Very old people		
An unemployed neighbor		
A naughty child		
A very drunk person		
A bank robber		
An extremist		
Christ nailed to the cross		
A general		
A meditating person		
A pile of banknotes		
A bunch of psychology books		
The Bible		
People who beat each other		
A devious person		
Sunshine		
Heavy rain		
A lonely mountain valley		
Two loving people		
A highly polished car		
Bank hall		
Alien family as neighbors		
A person who does nothing		
A beach crowed with people		
Underground railway		
Train ride to work		
A kilometer-long traffic jam		
Nuclear Waste Storage		
Rowboat ride on the lake		
Climber on the rock		
Two boxers in a fight		
Two people kissing		
"Red light" milieu		
Many dead fish on a lake shore		
A blooming meadow		
Office space with many plants		
Tax office		
A fine meal		
Historical ruins (castles)		
A failure		

Picture, emotional Reaction:	Experience:	Value (pos./neg.):
An aggressive motorist		
A retirement home		
A coffin		
A birth		
A defiant child		
A domineering woman		
An angry screaming man		
A lonely young woman		
An ambulance with siren		
A classroom		
A psychoanalyst, psychologist		
A pastor		
A primary school teacher		
A bouquet		
Meditation music		
Someone in relaxation exercise		
A professor		
Director-General of a bank		
Slum life scenario		
A happy young couple		
A happy mid-fifties man		
A desperate in front of a pension		
A wise man		
A sexually excited man		

Notes and Perspectives

How does man (on average) capture the aspects of his feelings?

Write down the key words in this subchapter:

What causes a little conscious and differentiated emotional experience?

Reflecting on what triggers feelings is essential because:

What did you learn about the components of emotions in your parents' home, school, and church?

What meaning, when living together, has the conversation about the effects of feelings?

Which aspects of feelings are 'allowed' in politics and the economy?

What does advertising convey about the value of feelings?

Formulate an important question for the subjective experience of feeling:

4.1.3. The dealing with feelings

How should man live with his emotional diversity? Many cannot cope with their feelings. They are dominated by their moods and current feelings.

One's feelings shape its thinking, values, and personal behavior. This is often like a 'rollercoaster': up and down, back and forth, high and low. This urges everyone to look for solutions.

One person might think that feelings are dangerous or 'bad' for life. As a result, that person no longer perceives them, oppresses them, and finds a 'balance' in work and leisure activities. Others live their feelings emphasized, but one-sided, in resolving to a certain emotional state every day. Others unload their emotions relentlessly in their environment.

Some argue that one must consciously cultivate feelings in all life situations, e.g. at work, at school and in relationships. One should not hurt one another's feelings, many say. Is not it true that life offers many moments each day in which feelings are violated, be it by human beings, by laws, by the built environment, by workplace conditions or by noise and stench?

How should man deal with his feelings? Are there constructive ways? Dealing with feelings can be learned. This does not mean that stressful feelings should "technically" be overwhelmed.

The first approach is simple: control the external influencing factors more and if necessary, avoid them.

A second way is the "psycho-hygiene": with relaxation and mental training to balance the psychic energy and bring the thoughts to rest.

A third way is the conscious way of life and with that a positive attitude towards burdening feelings. This means: to affirm and understand feelings.

Anyone who knows the causes of his feelings can better deal with them, and clarify its roots, e.g. by coping to terms with the past. Because many new feelings activate earlier experiences. This results in an unnecessary reinforcement.

Anyone who has cleared up the unconscious is no longer feeling bound by his past, even in new situations that are like earlier ones.

There is no reasonable theory that says and justifies that you should live out every feeling in full force, or even increase it. A moderate and appropriate self-control and self-discipline is part of a constructive approach to emotions.

Everyone can learn to manage his feelings. Positive feelings can be built up through education and individuation.

The goal of life, however, is hardly "always having positive feelings".

Reflections and Discussion

Appropriate treatment of feelings is possible when the "thing" that has triggered a feeling is made aware. Feelings are not simply "without reason".

You can rarely just "make positive feelings". The other way around: Negative feelings cannot usually be changed like a shirt, from gray black to yellow orange.

One can also create feelings 'artificially', with oneself as with others.

Many circumstances from different areas can trigger emotions. These include:

☐ Personal events   ☐ Social relations
☐ Actions of the person   ☐ Inner psychic situation
☐ Circumstances   ☐ Tangible objects
☐ A strange events

There are some positive feelings that all human beings would like to experience, e.g. joy, hope, contentment, self-confidence, well-being, "I"-strength, and love. Such feelings only become stable and sustainable through deepened self-education.

Positive feelings can be built up and negative feelings can be broken down. To deal with feelings means:

☐ Note needs   ☐ Clarify the unconscious
☐ Look at dreams   ☐ Take feelings seriously
☐ Keep self-control conscious   ☐ Do something in life
☐ Take a closer look at the thinking process
☐ Select external influences   ☐ Change life situations.
☐ Look carefully at emotional diversity   ☐ Reflect lifestyle
☐ Understand the psychodynamics   ☐ Practice fitness
☐ Take nutrition seriously

Emotions are obviously not a coincidence. Nor are they to be understood as the weather. At the same time, it is hardly a goal to want to persist in a "happy emotional state" steadily.

Negative feelings are also part of life, such as cleaning, cooking, eating, washing, sleeping, working and so on.

The aim is to learn to handle everything correctly.

Diagram 4.1.3: Dealing with emotions

Diagramm OS6-3: Mit Gefühlen umgehen

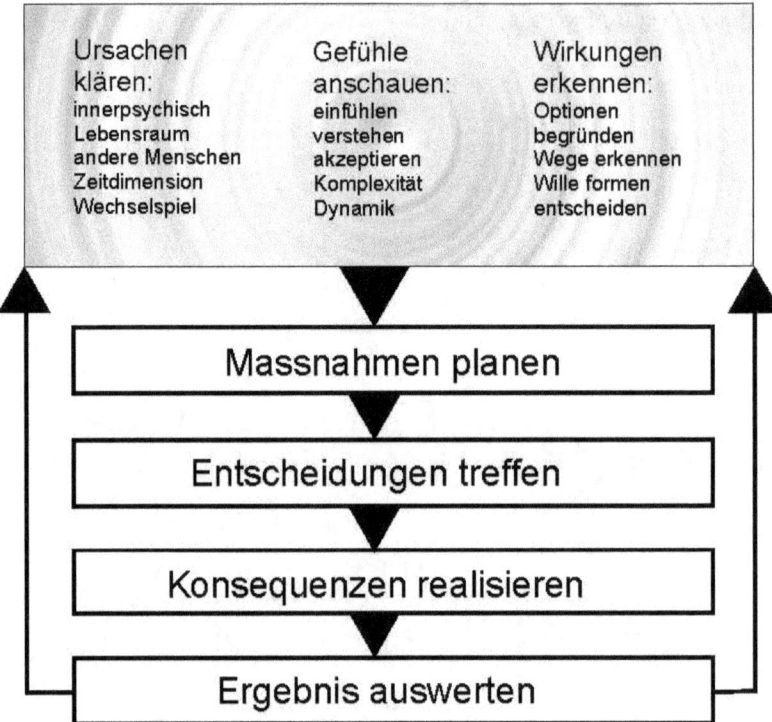

English Translation: **Clearing causes:** inner-psychical, habitat, other humans, time dimension, interplay & **Looking at emotions:** empathizing, understanding, accepting, complexity, dynamic & **Identifying effects:** justifying options, distinguishing ways, forming will, deciding > **Planning steps** > **Taking a decision** > **Realizing consequences** > **Evaluating the result** which retroacts.

The indirect handling of emotions

The idea that man can always control his feelings, (e.g. he should always keep them under the control of the mind, if possible living in equanimity, unmoved by ups and downs of feelings) is wrong.

The care of one's own feelings is essential. Feelings are a fundamental part of life and can be experienced as both positive and negative.

Practical suggestions to help with your emotions include:

☐ Thoughts that you suppress become particularly active and break through into emotions. Therefore, deal with your 'thoughts'.

☐ Worries are part of the 'normal' life. If you suppress them, or trivialize what worries you, then the feelings of worry break through indirectly. Therefore, take your worries seriously!

☐ Even smaller general fears can build up over time, e.g., to become incapable of making a decision. Therefore, search for the reasons of feelings of anxiety!

☐ Feelings are often difficult till impossible to control. Here is the wrong approach. Therefore, when you recognize what triggers your feelings, you should start there!

☐ Unfinished things and pending activities cause inner tensions and often fears. When a process is completed, it brings satisfaction and inner peace. Therefore, learn on the one hand to be able to put certain things on the ice internally (e.g. set priorities!) and on the other hand, do unfinished activities to a schedule!

☐ Some feelings of insecurity arise because the methodological meanings are not clear, lacking competences (e.g. communication skills). Therefore, clarify what competences you lack and learn them!

☐ If we explain and justify an event incorrectly, the wrong feelings (e.g. the causes seeing in one's own or supposing as immutable) will arise Therefore, be careful and check exactly your explanations, and in general, your explanatory style (See conflicts as a positive opportunity)!

☐ Anyone who (at home and at workplace) always thinks that everything must be in line with his ideas, creates massive internal pressure. Therefore, check and change your settings in this case!

☐ It may be right to do certain things 'perfectly', mostly this can be overwhelming to yourself, the others, and the thing itself. Therefore, personal satisfaction, can usually be expected with 90% performance quality.

☐ Images significantly affect our lives and create feelings accordingly. On the one hand, fantasies are activated by unconscious material, on the other hand there is also the 'play with the fantasies'. Therefore, keep a certain psycho-hygiene with the feelings and do not always let all images run wild!

☐ Every human must learn to live with defects. Idealistic ideas often create massive internal pressure and corresponding feelings of dissatisfaction. Therefore, recognize the positive challenge on the one hand and on the other you acquire appropriate demands on life!

☐ Too strong experience of success often stresses on relationships and disproportionately demands the emotional life. Therefore, it is wise not to overstate material and business success.

☐ Too intensive work-oriented people, usually with an exaggerated sense of duty, create themself feelings of frustration because their 'inner man' cannot live. Excessive admiration, addiction, and greed create as much suffering as violence! Therefore, keep self-reflection critical and allow yourself 'life'!

☐ A mismatch between social position and mental-spiritual development destroys every healthy emotional life!

Using introspection to approach feelings

Introspection is a direct way to identify, understand and transform one's own feelings. We are guided by psychoanalytic reflections to this method and present some considerations that can help familiarize with introspection.

Introspection means: looking at the physical and mental realm inside oneself or into other people or things, looking through, regard with an attentive regardful observation. Introspection is a feeling, touching, sensing of the inner state.

Psychoanalysis primarily means systematic introspection, strong veraciousness and self-discipline to achieve a comprehensive self-knowledge.

The aim of introspection is to uncover the unconscious. It is used to discover introspectively: defense mechanisms, ideals, suffering, potentials, impulses, conflicts, the superego and 'neurotic elements'.

Introspection makes it possible to deal thoroughly with one's own past and the unconscious present.

Self-analysis is the form of introspection. It drives the need for truthfulness to analytical self-exploration. As a precondition for self-exploration, one must first become physically and mentally quiet, relaxed, and concentrated.

Self-analysis is a way of introspection, a possibility to clean up and to prepare the inner space, to free it that other things can happen.

A human being ceases to be human when he no longer observes himself and always seeks rest and food in the outside.

Introspection as a self-questioning, self-reflection, self-knowledge, and self-assessment is an everyday human behavior to himself. We do not investigate an inner abstract hollow, but consider a concrete present action, think concretely about what we have done or want to do.

Introspection is self-assurance about how things stood, stand, will stand about oneself. Therefore, introspection enables a conscious lifestyle.

Introspection is not just thinking but acting and reacting to the self in the breadth of its possibilities: Grief, regret, disappointment over loss and failure, happiness in a present success, fear or hope in view of other probabilities. Introspection means "know thyself". It also means contemplation of its origin from the divine, knowledge of God. Introspection also means:

"Do not lose yourself in the outside, go back into yourself, inside the truth lives. And then, when you discover that your being is changeable, exceed yourself, but keep in mind that you are crossing a spirit-thinking soul. Consequently, go where the light of the Spirit shines.

Notes and Perspectives

How does man (on average) deal with his feelings?

Write down the key words in this subchapter:

What causes indifference to one's own feelings?

The deliberately reflected handling of emotions is essential because:

What did you learn about introspection in the home, school, and church?

What meaning in living together has the conversation about dealing with feelings?

How are feelings handled in politics and the economy?

What does advertising convey about introspection?

Formulate an important question for you to build positive feelings:

4.1.4. Exercises

1. Looking back over the past few weeks, how is the spectrum of your feelings?

2. How do you deal with your feelings in everyday life?

3. What 'value' do you have for your feelings, compared to how you think and act?

4. How do your feelings affect your thoughts, decisions, and actions?

5. How do you get to the bottom of your feelings?

6. How do you want other people to handle your emotional life?

7. How do other people's feelings affect you?

8. How important is the emotional life of those around you.

9. Mood. Weekly Review

6= heavy   5 = very   4 = distinct   3 = moderate   2 = low   1 = hardly

9.a) Pleasant:

	Mo	Thu	Wed	Thu	Fri	Sat	Sun
Well:							
Relaxed:							
Warm:							
Harmoniously:							
Calm:							
Animated:							
Fulfilled:							
Open:							

Interpret causes:

What are the effects?

9.a) Unpleasant:

	Mo	Thu	Wed	Thu	Fri	Sat	Sun
Unwell:							
Tense:							
Cold:							
Disrupted:							
Restless:							
'Stopped':							
Unfulfilled:							
Locked:							

Interpret causes:

What are the effects?

9.c) General conclusions (measures):

10.a) The profile of one's own feelings: Look back on the last days and weeks. Try to keep track of your emotional variety according to the given list.

Note in the empty column:
(almost) always = 4 / frequently = 3 / sometimes = 2 / little = 1 / never = 0

Positive feeling:	Frequency:	Negative feeling:	Frequency:
Ur-confidence		Anxiety	
Fulfilled		Emptiness	
Peace		Strife	
Harmony		Disharmony	
Truthfulness		Denial	
Love		Hate	
Participation		Alienation	
Security		Uncertainty	
Connectedness		Loneliness	

Satisfaction		Discontent	
Wholeness		Disruption	
Meaningfulness		Futility	
Freedom		Bondage	
Happiness		Unhappiness	
Hope		Hopelessness	
Trust		Distrust	
Vitality		Depressed	
Joy		Joyless	
Dedication		Aggression	
Total:		**Total:**	

10.b) Causes of feelings: Try to complete the given list with a keyword, where possible causes are:

Positive feeling:	Causes	Negative feeling:	Causes
Ur-confidence		Anxiety	
Fulfilled		Emptiness	
Peace		Strife	
Harmony		Disharmony	
Truthfulness		Denial	
Love		Hate	
Participation		Alienation	
Security		Uncertainty	
Connectedness		Loneliness	
Satisfaction		Discontent	
Wholeness		Disruption	
Meaningfulness		Futility	
Freedom		Bondage	
Happiness		Unhappiness	
Hope		Hopelessness	
Trust		Distrust	
Vitality		Depressed	
Joy		Joyless	
Dedication		Aggression	

Formulate three suggestions about actions what you can do to eliminate negative causes and create a positive emotional state:

Multiple Choice Test

Select the four correct answers:

7.1. The spectrum of feelings. Central statements are:

- ☐ a) There are many different expressions of giving life.
- ☐ b) Unpleasant feelings are always negative.
- ☐ c) Feelings also express a certain experience of being.
- ☐ d) There are people who can live without feelings.
- ☐ e) Feelings are an indispensable part of being human
- ☐ f) Emotions are always the experience of formed psychic energy.

7.2. The characteristics of the emotions. Characteristics of emotions are:

- ☐ a) Value aspect
- ☐ b) Intensity
- ☐ c) Duration
- ☐ d) Uniqueness
- ☐ e) Feeling superposition
- ☐ f) Simplicity

7.3. Dealing with the feelings. You can change feelings by:

- ☐ a) Relating meaning
- ☐ b) Living out feelings
- ☐ c) Empathizing
- ☐ d) Changing the trigger
- ☐ e) Clarifying the way of life
- ☐ f) Reflecting

4.2. The Complex Functions of Feelings

4.2.1. The categorization of emotions

We can divide feelings according to different points of view. First, we experience feelings as 'positive' or 'negative'.

This includes a personal valuation, because not every feeling means the same value for everyone in all situations. Experiencing mourning can be considered as a positive feeling. Dissatisfaction or fear are feelings that are experienced negatively but may well have constructive aspects.

Secondly, 'positive' or 'negative' is often equated with pleasant or unpleasant. But even a feeling of aggression or anger can be liberating in expressions and in this sense 'pleasant'.

Sometimes the short-term desire is pleasant, but actually rather negative, for example because more important things are being brushed away.

Third, there are feelings that are more physical and others more 'spiritual' experienced. Tenderness and well-being are experienced more body related, while joy and truthfulness are feelings of sense-fulfillment and value-experience.

Fourth, there are feelings that have a material (worldly) relation, while others are psychologically oriented. 'Safety' can be experienced in a car and in a relationship. 'Harmony' and a feeling of 'wholeness' refer more to the experience of psychological forces than of externalities.

A fifth categorization is "subject-related" and "object-related". Here, however, are meant more the emotional factors that can be inside or outside; a feeling that is experienced close to oneself or primary related to the external.

Sixth, we can distinguish 'repulsive' and 'attractive' feelings. Antipathy and enmity push for avoidance, while sympathy and friendship activate attention.

Seventh, feelings can also be viewed from the point of view of constructiveness or destructiveness. Some feelings contain both aspects. Thus, a burst of anger for the inner discharge, and thus be positive for health, but is seen as negative in most cases and has in the interactions usually a destructive effect.

A general classification is hardly possible. The interpretation of feelings varies from person to person and from culture to culture.

Reflections and Discussion

Aspects of the classification are:
- Positive-negative
- Close to the body and spirit
- Subject-related and object-related
- Constructive-destructive
- Pleasant-unpleasant
- Factual and mentally
- Attractive-repulsive

The experience of feelings always includes an interpretation according to:
- Approved or disapproved by others
- In combination with the situation
- Under the perspective of the past and the future
- According to cultural 'customs'
- Desired or not desired
- In relation to other feelings

The profile of one's own feelings: It is sensible and constructive to look back on the last days and weeks and to capture the variety of emotions.

Positive feeling:	Frequency	Negative feeling:	Frequency
Ur-confidence		Anxiety	
Fulfilled		Emptiness	
Peace		Strife	
Harmony		Disharmony	
Truthfulness		Denial	
Love		Hate	
Participation		Alienation	
Security		Uncertainty	
Connectedness		Loneliness	
Satisfaction		Discontent	
Wholeness		Conflictive	
Meaningfulness		Futility	
Freedom		Bondage	
Happiness		Unhappiness	
Hope		Hopelessness	
Trust		Distrust	
Vitality		Depressed	
Joy		Joyless	
Dedication		Aggression	

Make an average profile of people's feelings in the group.

Diagram 4.2.1: The experiencing of emotions

Diagramm OS6-4: Das Erleben der Gefühle

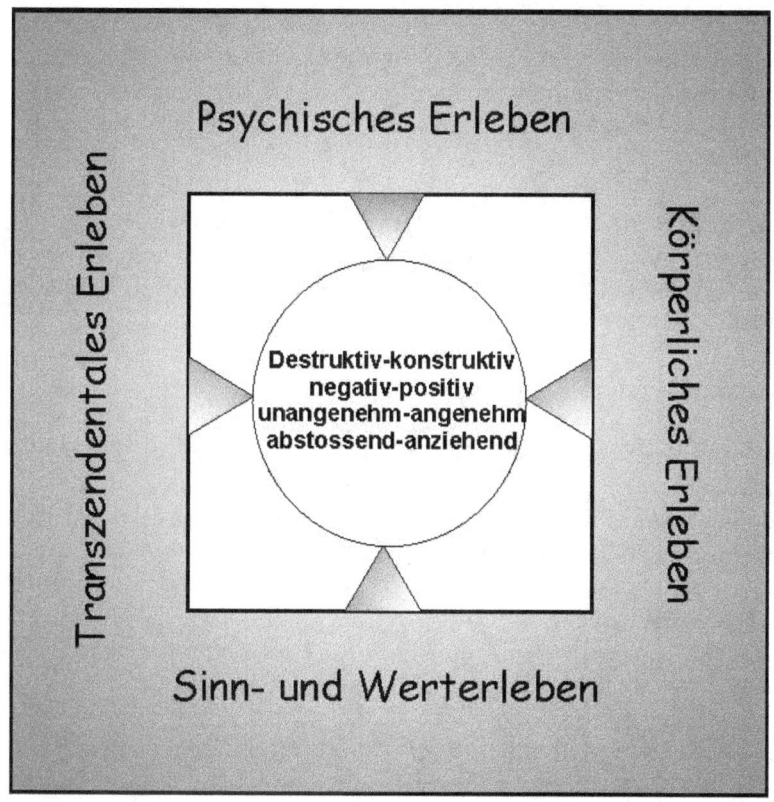

English Translation: **The experiencing of emotions** is composed of **Psychological experience & Physical experience & Experience of sense and value & Transcendental experience** interacting destructive – constructive, negative – positive, painful – pleasant, repellant – attractive.

4.2.2. Emotional expression & emotional development

Emotions have many forms of expression. We can recognize a feeling from facial expressions and gestures. A happy face looks different from an angry one. Anyone who is sorrowful or enthusiastic will show a specific gesture. Emotions have bodily experienced side effects.

Feelings affect processes in the brain, the circulatory system, respiration, and the nervous and glandular systems. Fear, as well as hope and joy, produces physiological reactions. Expressive and motor, we can recognize the power of emotions.

Many actions are not simply the result of a thinking process or a habit or a skill, but fundamentally influenced by the psychical energy and meaning of current feelings. Emotions express themselves above all in thinking and in speech.

We accentuate three central expressions:

Everyone experiences his feelings as pleasant or unpleasant and in this sense as positive or negative, as constructive or destructive. The pleasant is soothing, stimulating, liberating and attractive. The unpleasant is repulsive, restrictive, exciting, and oppressive.

Then we have the power of a feeling. Some feelings are rather weak, superficial, bland and seem 'empty' or powerless. Other feelings have a strong energy. They are intense, heightened, moving and violent.

And finally, time is another aspect of expression. Some emotions are short-lived, others have a long-lasting effect.

Many times, and at the same time, the human being has different feelings that overlap, amplify, or contradict one another, e.g. can even be in opposition to each other. It comes down to a struggle for power. Weaker feelings disappear or are pushed back for a while.

Feelings can also strengthen each other and be experienced in a new form more intense in strength and quality. An interest becomes an enthusiasm, then a joy and finally a deep feeling of happiness. A "bad mood" leads to sorrow, then to aggression and finally to rage and anger.

Reflections and Discussion

Feelings have physiological effects:

Brain, e.g.:	
Nerves, e.g.:	
Breathing, e.g.:	
Circulation, e.g.:	
Glands, e.g.:	

Feelings have different expressions:

Pleasant, e.g.	
Unpleasant, e.g.	
Intensity, e.g.	
Weakness, e.g.	
Duration, e.g.	

Feelings can increase:

Positive mutually reinforcing feelings are:	
Negative mutually reinforcing feelings are:	
Emotions can collide:	

A daily log of emotional state sometimes helps, always serves self-knowledge.

Emotional expression Day time	pleasant unpleasantly	strong weak	longer shorter
Morning			
Late morning			
Mid-day			
Afternoon			
Eve			
Night			

Observe your fellow human beings in everyday life and create an average profile in the group together.

Diagram 4.2.2: Compacting & overlaying of emotions

Diagramm OS6-5: Die Verdichtung und Ueberlagerung der Gefühle

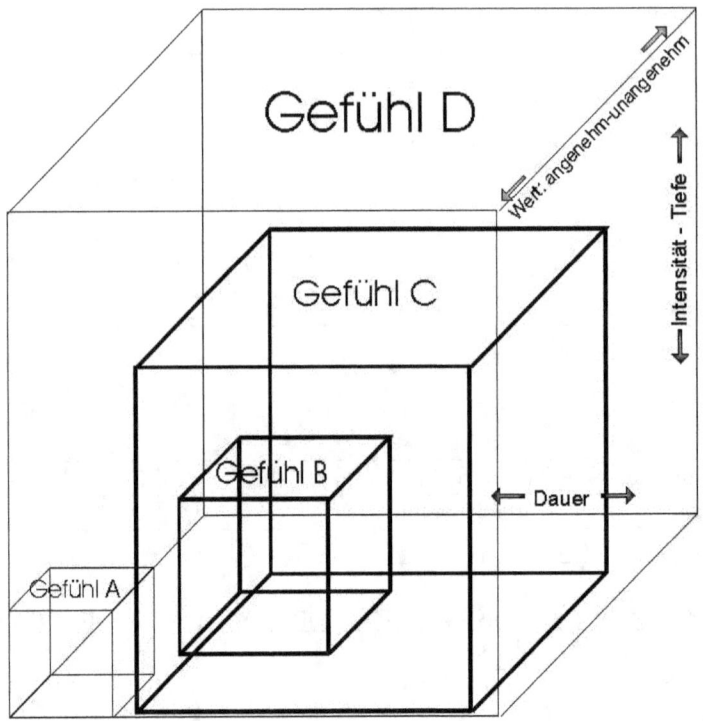

English Translation: Emotion A, Emotion B, Emotion C, Emotion D interact in the dimensions of **duration, intensity - depth, value: pleasant-unpleasant**

4.2.3. Feeling-activating forces

Many external and intrapsychic factors can trigger emotions. Below are six aspects:

Firstly, through their actions, often through their presence, people can cause another person's feelings. Humans can value others, give them pleasure, take them seriously, support them and treat them benevolently. The opposite is also a reality: scoff at others, humiliate, exploit, deceive, weaken, or reject.

Second, objects from the habitat create multiple emotions. There are many pleasure-producing products, helpful machines, inviting rooms, and simply, 'beautiful' things! Negative emotions can also be triggered by things such as dirt, noise, anonymous buildings, and 'inhumanly' built-up areas.

Third, living conditions can trigger emotions. Pleasant feelings people experience in good living conditions, conflict-free relationships, enough money and security. Worries, hardships and unfavorable living conditions almost always trigger negative feelings.

Fourth, particularly 'critical' events are emotion-activating. The death of a loved one, the dissolution of a shared life, unemployment, illness and much more create deep stressful feelings. On the other hand, birth, marriage, a feast, a gift, a success, can bring more powerful positive feelings.

Fifth, the intrapsychic situation is to be mentioned. The unprocessed past can be a heavy burden. A strict superego and brooding thoughts are oppressive. Suppressed anger, feelings of inferiority or insecurity create negative moods. Confident thoughts, on the other hand, or the experience of inner freedom, generate positive feelings. A strong willpower, a factually differentiated self-confidence and experiencing the inner growth cause life-like and creatively stimulating feelings.

Sixth, social conditions must be considered. Racism, violence, crime, recession and above all warlike events, experienced in one's own country or on television, often burden emotional life more than is perceived. On the other hand, peace, social security, freedom, and a prosperous economic life can decisively shape many people in their basic mood.

Reflections and Discussion

The most diverse areas of life can trigger feelings. Write down some examples from the conversation with others:

- ☐ People:
- ☐ Tangible objects:
- ☐ Living situation:
- ☐ Personal events:
- ☐ Inner-psychic powers:
- ☐ National / international situation:

Every day a person can experience the most diverse elements from all areas, which together create a 'melody' of emotions. These include:

- ☐ Different and opposing elements
- ☐ Almost simultaneously, person-close and person-foreign facts
- ☐ The basic mood overlying influences
- ☐ Regular impulse action, e.g. through advertising and news
- ☐ Fact-related and human-related factors side by side

Choose factors / elements from the six areas that affect many people almost every day. Discuss the longer-term effects in the group, note an item, and the impact:

- ☐ People:
- ☐ Tangible objects:
- ☐ Living situation:
- ☐ Personal events:
- ☐ Inner-psychic powers:
- ☐ Inter- / national situation:

Group work: What are the most important long-term effects of the many influencing factors on people?

Diagram 4.2.3: Emotion-activating conditions

Diagramm OS6-6: Gefühlsaktivierende Gegebenheiten

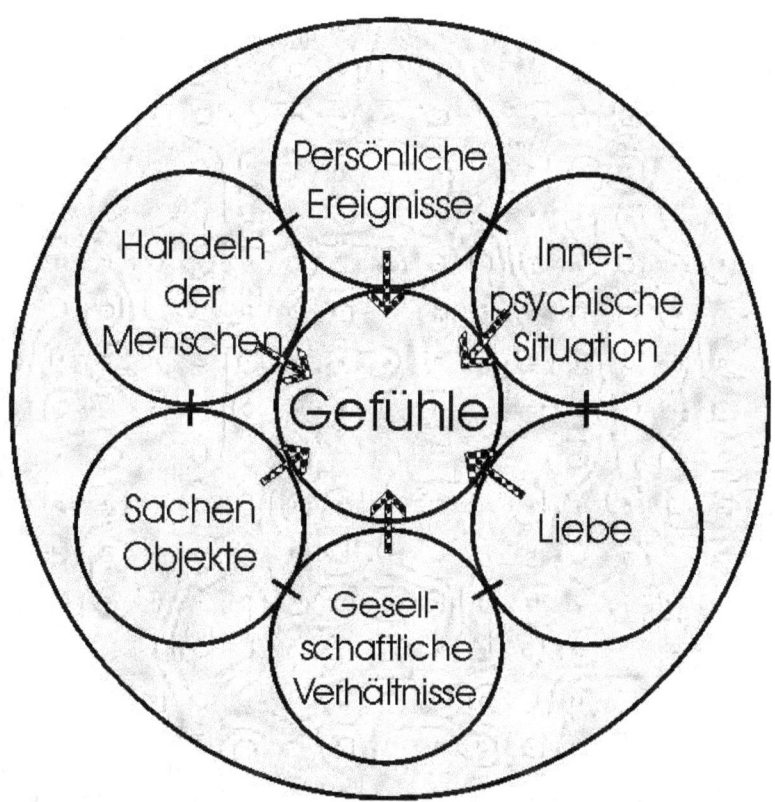

English Translation: Emotions are influenced in interactions by Individual incident, Inner-psychical situation, Love, Social circumstances, Things & objects, The acting of humans

4.2.4. The effects of feelings

Emotions have all-round effects. They influence perception and, at the same time, they value the experience. The thought processes are also influenced by feelings. Many value judgments are based more on feelings than on factual arguments. The body is affected by feelings.

Strong feelings affect the respiration, the circulation, the nerves, the digestion, the brain, and the glands. Thus, the bodily needs, especially physiological needs, are activated or disturbed. A grief can take away hunger. Frustration often pushes for food. The psychical needs are activated or suppressed depending on the emotional state. The power of love is more than a feeling: it is a performance. This ability diminishes the more negative the feelings are. Those who are angry, fearful, or oppressed, have little power to reconcile, to work for others or to do something, even if they are positive values.

Feelings also influence the phantasy and the imagination. Often the themes of the emotions show through in dreams. Religious beliefs are mostly based on feelings for most people.

Man can suppress his feelings, heat up or integrate them into the "I"-guidance. Once emotions are there, they are a reality that is not easy to get rid of or maintain long term.

Man is required to face his emotional world if he does not want to be controlled by his feelings. At first, this self-encounter is not about a judgmental rejection, but about acceptance and understanding.

Emotions decisively 'make' a person's personal life. They determine the course of a relationship. They shape politics. They are the forces that cause violence, oppression, and wars. What can cause "blind rage" is known. Hate and greed, envy and jealousy are the emotional forces that can guide humans and people into dramas.

Anyone who understands his feelings and integrates them into the "I" guidance has recognized the variety of effects and the abundance of triggering factors.

Reflections and Discussion

Feelings work on:

Perception	Beliefs	Creativity	Love
Actions	Word choice	Facial expression	Need
Thinking	Body	Phantasy	

Emotions, as well as thinking, can be integrated into the ego leadership. For example:

- ☐ Emotions can be suppressed
- ☐ Feelings can be distributed postponed
- ☐ Feelings can be heated, exaggerated, 'inflated'
- ☐ Feelings can get out of control
- ☐ Feelings can be consciously cared for
- ☐ Feelings can be processed

Suppressed, heated-up, and letting gone feelings have different consequences. Make a list of your experiences:

In the "I" leadership integrated and processed feelings, create various positive effects. Generate some examples from your experience:

The effects of emotions are diverse and often reach all mental subsystems. Create an average picture in the group:

Emotion Effects	Sorrow	Joy	Rage	Interest	Hope
Phantasy					
Thinking					
Acting					
Love					
Needs					
Will					
Integration					

Diagram 4.2.4: Trigger of emotions and spheres

Diagramm OS6-7: Auslöser von Gefühlen und Wirkungsbereiche

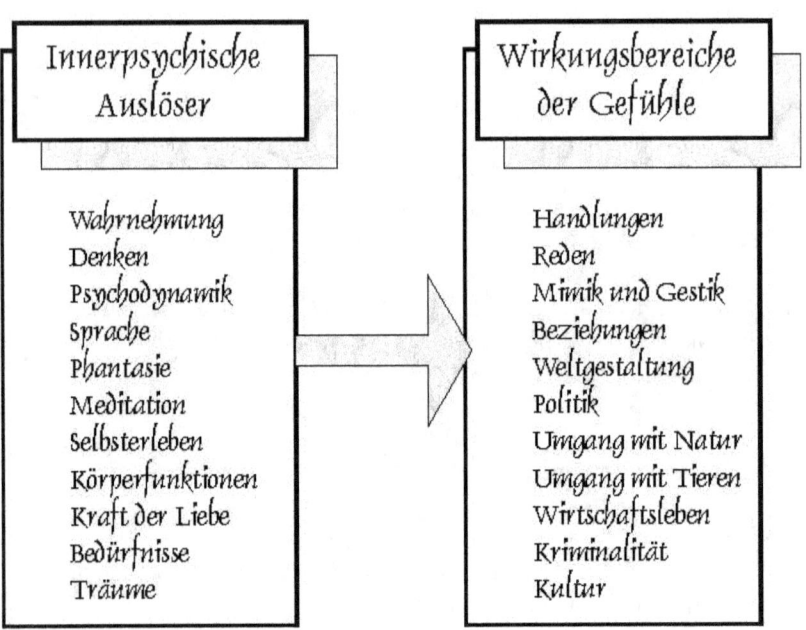

Innerpsychische Auslöser	Wirkungsbereiche der Gefühle
Wahrnehmung	Handlungen
Denken	Reden
Psychodynamik	Mimik und Gestik
Sprache	Beziehungen
Phantasie	Weltgestaltung
Meditation	Politik
Selbsterleben	Umgang mit Natur
Körperfunktionen	Umgang mit Tieren
Kraft der Liebe	Wirtschaftsleben
Bedürfnisse	Kriminalität
Träume	Kultur

English Translation:
Inner-psychical trigger: Perception, thinking psychodynamic, language, phantasy, meditation, self-experience, body-functions, power of love, needs, dreams > affect

Sphere of emotions: Actions, speaking, facial expression & gesture, relations, world-design, politics, handling with nature, handling with animals, economical life, criminality, culture

4.2.5. Sense and value experience

Emotions always contain a value aspect. An emotional experience is a value experience without value judgment, in a sense, concomitant to the 'vibration' of the feeling. Lust generally has a positive value. What is pleasantly experienced also means 'good'. Emotions are predominantly polarized in a value scale in this sense.

This experience of value is then transmitted in two directions: on the one hand to the feeling-inducing factors and on the other hand to the effect of the feeling. Thus, prosperity, health, security, happiness, and success acquire a positive value, without the individual is formulating a value in thinking.

What causes pain, inner suffering, burden, and pressure, is received as a negative value, even if consciously no value judgment is made. The experiencing of value is then transferred to the feeling-triggering reality, thus, adding value to the external realities. The "sympathetic person" receives a positive value, while the "unsympathetic person" receives a negative value quality. The same applies to social relationships, to things and to the inner-psychical life in general.

Because people emotionally experience the same reality with different feelings, the commitment value is variable in quality and intensity. Thus, an action receives primarily a judgement that corresponds to the feelings that are resulted from it. The emotional value experience is also subject to the process of education.

What is experienced as 'positively' valuable usually also receives a correspondingly positive meaning. Lust-fulfillment becomes meaningfulness. Anyone who experiences feelings mentally is more open to in the psycho-spiritual context.

Depending on their responsiveness, for example, esteem and self-realization have deep meaning for some, while others experience little 'sense' in it. For many, the question of meaning will be experienced when certain circumstances or events are experienced in a particularly 'critical' manner: "What is the use of meaning?" Some only experience it as a question of existence when positive feelings are lacking. Therefore, the experience of feeling becomes a meaningful life.

The purpose of a car is to have one and drive it. The sense of joy is: "I'm fine." Sense and value are approved as far as "good feelings" are included.

Reflections and Discussion

The experience of feelings is accompanied by a value experience:

☐ Hope: positive value because it is future-building, redemptive, and liberating.
☐ Sorrow: negative value because it can be stressful, constricting, and unpleasurable.

People experience things and circumstances in different ways, because they trigger different emotions in them:

☐ Lottery: to have, to hope, a new life, or, the eternal loser.
☐ Car: increase self-esteem, experience of freedom, or, environmental impact.

Sense experience depends strongly on the judgmental feeling experience:

☐ Tragic event: senseless, "only God knows the meaning", or, searching deeper
☐ Career: money, reputation, wealth, or, loss of inner autonomy.

Attitudes, beliefs, and value judgments are always based first on an emotional evaluative experience of the content. Moral teachings are rarely based on pure 'desk work'. The initial situation is evaluating of the emotional experience. This gives rise to value teachings and moral demands. There are innumerable such systems because people move away from reality in favor of emotional experience.

The sense and value experience can be explored in all areas of life; discuss in the group:

Areas	Nature Resources	God Transcendence	Mental Life	Society Environment
Basic emotional experience				
Basic values and meaning				
Values for Actions				
Prospective Evaluation				

Diagram 4.2.5: Aspects of sense & value of the experiencing emotions

Diagramm OS6-8: Die Sinn- und Wertaspekte des Gefühlserlebens

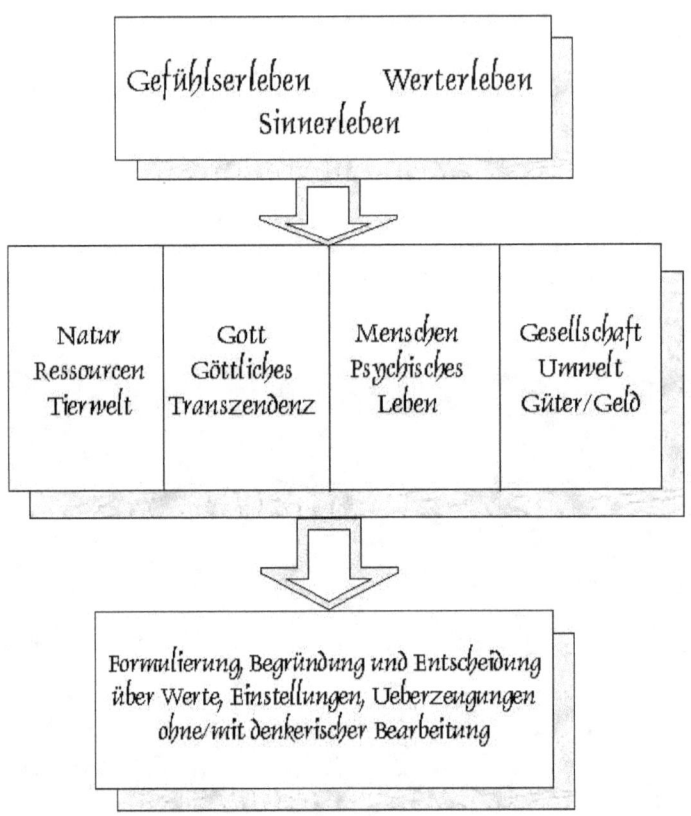

English Translation: Experiencing emotions, values & sense > influence on
Nature, resources, world of animals /God, divine, transcendence / Humans, psychical life / Society, environment, goods, money > effecting Formulation, justification and decision over values, attitudes, convictions without or with thinking processing.

4.2.6. The networking of emotions

In many cases, feelings are not isolated, but are linked with various other feelings, partly simultaneously, and partly in succession. Let's have a look on networking with the example "Aggression":

First is a direct cause: A hurt (slight) can dispose an aggressive mood, also privations, overexitations (Noise), little space (apartment), heteronomy, losing in favor of others, a difficulty in an action.

Then there is to consider the emotional shift: feeling of guilt can be masked with an aggressive mood. Frustrations and feelings of alienation often lead to aggressive feelings.

Impatience not to accept a difficult situation and changing in material conditions can dispose often aggressive mood. While some live this mood, others try to suppress it, or transform it religiously, or turn it into a positive action. This gives rise to new feelings. The possibilities are manifold: Increased guilt, despair, fainting, arrogance, psycho-somatic reactions, feelings of anxiety and so on.

Let us choose a positive example: Joy. This is more than a pleasant feeling, more than lust, more than fun or amusement. Joy has to do with the experience of love, be it experiencing affection, or be it your own lived love in an interaction. Joy contains self-confidence and the feeling of being valuable. Joy requires good relationships. Who, despite the many sorrowful conditions in the world (experience being), creates a positive world relationship, can feel joy of life.

Joy arises not only in the experience of certain situations but arises from a deep self-experience. A work result or creative activity can convey the feeling of joy. The body experience can activate joyful feelings.

Coziness and familiarity often go hand in hand with the feeling of joy. Human experiences joy when he realizes himself, recognizes inner growth, is interested in life, achieves something beyond his own interests, feels inwardly free and has found and lives his destiny (his purpose).

Reflections and Discussion

Many feelings are networked with others and 'play' the "main / supporting role".

☐ Hope: An interesting expectation, positive orientation, anticipated future, positive/ liberating surprise.

☐ Fear: Meaninglessness, suppressed feelings of guilt, blocked anger, experiencing a lack of love, threats, responsibility.

☐ Being oppressed: Existential pressure from the subconscious, sorrow, powerlessness, hopelessness.

☐ Self-confidence: Positive performance, appreciation, security, acceptance, praise, experience of willpower

☐ Anger: Hatred, dislike, disapproval, hostile thoughts, hurt, feelings of inferiority, humiliation

Many emotions are networked, and it is not often possible to distinguish one as the cause of another, as there are different effects.:

☐ Depression Causes: increased consumer behavior, pleasure-oriented experience, ritualized everyday life, fatalism, avoiding life, perfectionism, moods, tense relationships, indifference, adherence to things

☐ Joy brings: Lust for life, active life, a love of life, a feeling for the care of nature and wildlife, constructive relationships, reconciliation ability, strong sense of responsibility beyond oneself

Some emotions have objective components that can be addressed directly, for example, the feeling of guilt:

☐ Reviewing the superego and, if necessary, revising
☐ Extending action skills
☐ Taking responsibility for your own actions (and life)
☐ Formulating and justifying values (own standards)
☐ Setting goals and taking them step by step.
☐ Strengthen will by focusing on the wills parts
☐ Recognizing and taking back projections
☐ Processing the unconscious
☐ Effectively tackling situations with all your might

What are your 'critical' feelings now?

Discuss, with others, the possible networks, and ways to change:

Which existing positive feelings do you want to strengthen?

Discuss with others the possible networks and ways to strengthen them:

Diagram 4.2.6: The impetus of complex networked emotions

Diagramm OS6-9: Die Stosskraft komplex vernetzter Gefühle

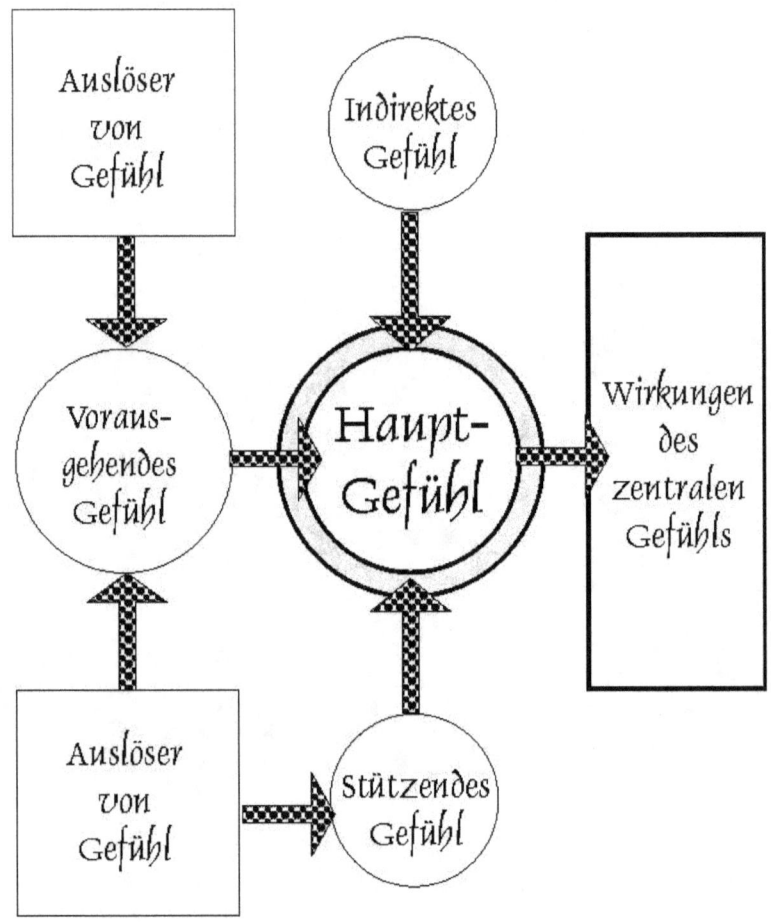

English Translation: **Trigger of emotion** affects
> **Prevenient emotion** and
> **Supporting emotion** and together with
> **Indirect emotion** the
> **Main emotion,** which influences
> **Effects of the central emotion.**

4.2.7. Working unit

4.2.7. Working unit - 1

1. a) How do you experience the diversity of emotions?

1. b) Expand the aspects of subjective interpretation of feelings:

2. a) The profile of one's own feelings: Look back on the last days and weeks; try to keep track of your emotional variety, according to the given list. Note in the empty column: 'common', 'sometimes', 'rare'.

Positive feeling:	Frequency	Negative feeling:	Frequency
Ur-confidence		Anxiety	
Fulfilled		Emptiness	
Peace		Strife	
Harmony		Disharmony	
Truthfulness		Denial	
Love		Hate	
Participation		Alienation	
Security		Uncertainty	
Connectedness		Loneliness	
Satisfaction		Discontent	
Wholeness		Disruption	
Meaningfulness		Futility	
Freedom		Bondage	
Happiness		Unhappiness	
Hope		Hopelessness	
Trust		Distrust	
Vitality		Depressed	
Joy		Joyless	
Dedication		Aggression	

2. b) Comment on and interpret your profile:

3. Formulate an educational goal for dealing with your emotional experiences:

4. a) Think about your feelings from an important situation. What were they?

4. b) Your conclusion in one sentence:

4.2.7. Working unit - 2

1. a) How do you experience the interaction between different feelings?

1. b) Extend the expressions of feelings with your observations:

2. a) Create a daily log of your emotional state:

Emotional expression Day time	pleasant unpleasantly	strong weak	longer shorter
Morning			
Late morning			
Mid-day			
Afternoon			
Eve			
Night			

2. b) Comment on the daily protocol:

3. Formulate an educational goal in the context of your general emotional expression:

4. a) What is your general way of expressing feelings?

4. b) Your conclusion in one sentence:

4.2.7. Working unit - 3

1. a) How do you experience the variety of emotional activating circumstances?

1. b) Comment on a sphere of life which especially activates feelings:

2. a) The most diverse areas of life can trigger emotions: Write down some examples from your own experience. Include elements / aspects in the following 6 areas:

☐ People:
☐ Tangible objects:
☐ Living situation:
☐ Personal events:
☐ Inner-psychic powers:
☐ National / international situation:

2. b) What do you conclude from 2. a) for you?

3. Formulate an educational goal in the context of emotion-activating forces:

4. a) Imagine a circumstance that causes you strong feelings:

4. b) Your conclusion in one sentence:

4.2.7. Working unit - 4

1. a) How do you experience the effects of positive emotions?

1. b) How do you experience the effects of negative feelings?

1. c) Extend the considerations on the effects of non-integrated feelings:

2. a) Make a note of your experiences on the effects of feelings with keywords:

Emotion Effects	Sorrow	Joy	Rage	Interest	Hope
Phantasy					
Thinking					
Acting					
Love					
Needs					
Will					
Integration					

2. b) Your conclusion:

3. Formulate an educational goal for the negative feelings:

4. a) Imagine your strongest negative feeling:

4. b) Your conclusion in one sentence:

4.2.7. Working unit - 5

1. a) How do you experience meaning and values related to the feelings?

1. b) What is the individual difference between a feeling and the meaning life?

2. a) Explore the meaning and value in your life experiences; give examples:

Areas	Nature Resources	God Transcendence	Mental Life	Society Environment
Basic emotional experience				
Basic values and meaning				
Values for Actions				
Prospective Evaluation				

2. Formulate a value judgment:

3. Formulate an educational goal for your general Inner Life:

4. a) Consider the meaning and value of your feelings:

4. b) Your conclusion in one sentence:

4.2.7. Working unit - 6

1. a) What are the links when you experience yourself aggressively?

1. b) Expand the relationships of anger with other feelings:

2. Provide some tips on how to handle these feelings in the following examples:

2. a) Feelings of inferiority:

2. b) Meaningless:

2. c) Mourning:

2. d) Aggression:

3. Formulate an educational goal in the context of aggressive emotions:

4. a) Imagine your aggressive feelings:

4. b) Your conclusion in one sentence:

4.2.7. Working unit - 7

Reflect critically: "You only have to have positive feelings, then luck and success come by themselves ....":

Multiple Choice Test

Select the four correct answers:

8.1. Feelings can be considered from the following points of view:
- ☐ a) Close to the body-spiritually
- ☐ b) Attractive or repellent
- ☐ c) Constructive or destructive
- ☐ d) Internal logic
- ☐ e) Physiological
- ☐ f) Pleasantly or unpleasant

8.2. Which of the following statements apply?
- ☐ a) Emotions often have a physiological effect.
- ☐ b) Feelings can be strengthened or weakened.
- ☐ c) Not every person has feelings.
- ☐ d) Emotions can overlap and / or transform into others.
- ☐ e) Feelings have different time intervals.
- ☐ f) The intensity of feelings is always subjectively justified.

8.3. Feelings are triggered by:
- ☐ a) Other people
- ☐ b) Things / objects
- ☐ c) Living conditions
- ☐ d) Inner experience
- ☐ e) Thinking operations
- ☐ f) Body movements

8.4. Emotions usually work on:
- ☐ a) Dreams
- ☐ b) Dealing with duties
- ☐ c) Perception
- ☐ d) Value judgments
- ☐ e) Need experience
- ☐ f) Fantasies

8.5. Meaning and value experiences contains with most humans:
- ☐ a) Rational analysis
- ☐ b) Personal experiences
- ☐ c) God like experience
- ☐ d) Emotional experience
- ☐ e) Emotional value experience
- ☐ f) Educational experience

8.6. Feelings are mostly networked with:
- ☐ a) Previous feelings
- ☐ b) Accompanying (secondary) feelings
- ☐ c) Practical experience
- ☐ d) Effects of feelings
- ☐ e) Trigger of feelings
- ☐ f) I-ideal

5. Psychodynamics and Psychic Energy

Essential theses

Each person activates and forms with his thoughts and feelings psychical energy.

The psychical energy is a psycho-energetic organism in the body, with different energy centers and appropriate outward radiation.

The psychical energy acts on the body organs, as it is formed according to thoughts, feelings, the unconscious, and so on.

Excessively tense psychical energy burdens the functions of the psychical forces and interferes with all actions.

Excessively tense psychical energy burdens the body (the organs) and has a disturbing or pathogenic effect.

Regular relaxation has a positive effect on the psychical energy, the body, and the acting.

5.1. The Invisible Psychical Energy

5.1.1. The psychical energy

Who says, "I could tear out trees now"? seldom means his physical strength, but rather his life energy. Worries are often experienced as a 'weight'. Both negative and positive thoughts have a significant effect on the attitude to life.

Many people experience telepathic phenomena: One thinks of someone or wants to make a phone call to a friend and a few minutes later the telephone rings. Or, you are invited to a visit; but, on your way, you have "a feeling in your stomach", is a kind of advance announcement that something is not going to be good there.

If you concentrate your eyes on the neck of a person in a public transport, then this person suddenly looks back or scratches his head. Nervousness and inner tension are contagious.

Anyone who empathizes with someone else's suffering often absorbs this suffering emotionally. If someone begins to cry violently after being severely blocked, then one can feel the energetic "emotional output" in full intensity.

Even whims create an energetic atmosphere. Where people with aggressive feelings have stayed, their "mood" in the air is still noticeable.

Pictures and colors do not only affect the eyes. They enliven the psychic energy inside. Anyone who sees pictures with his eyes closed will experience an energetic effect, dependent on what is seen, e.g. a sun, a dark forest, a deep blue night sky with stars or fantasies of all kinds.

TV advertising is designed to get psychic energy into motion with images and colors, and with music. An exciting novel and an action film can force the entire psychic energy to high tension. If you look at boxing or wrestling, you will experience your psychic energy accordingly: banged, shaken, and knocked down. A film about love can produce quite different energetic vibrations.

An experiment: A test subject sits in the circle of four to six people. They think inwardly: "Go away. We do not want you here". Or, "We are glad that you are with us". The person in the middle will feel the thought energy.

A husband can prepare himself for a quarrel with his wife, by thinking about everything he wants to reproach her on the way home. And vice versa: Positive thoughts precede and announce what is coming.

Hand and arm movements can be used to form and activate psychic energy. It can also act at a distance on the psycho-energetic system of other people.

Reflections and Discussion

There is psychic energy in everyone's body. We experience this kind of energy in many ways:

- Vitality: stimulated or blocked life energy.
- Active pleasure or lethargy
- Basic conditions: from well-being to oppression
- Physically as: pressure on the chest, shortness of breath, or anxiety,
- 'Knots' in the stomach, tension, or nervousness
- In feelings: joy, trust, love, aggression, grief, fear, etc

Generally known and scientifically proven:

- Pictorial thoughts form psychic energy
- Experience activates psychic energy
- The physical condition affects the psychic energy
- The unconscious binds psychic energy
- Needs purposefully arouse psychical energy
- The willpower concentrates psychic energy
- Action moves psychical energy
- Love sets psychic energy in motion

The psychical energy in man is a kind of "subtle body":

- The psychical energy in the human is a unity and wholeness with different energy centers (e.g. in the head, in the chest, in the stomach).
- The various psychological subsystems and forces activate and shape psychical energy into a complex energy field in the body.
- Psychical energy radiates outwards.
- Outside of man, there is a psychical energy that can guide the human-formed psychical energy over long distances. We know this as telepathy / clairvoyance.
- People can exert influence each other psycho energetically.

Psychical energy acts in the same way as the psychical powers in the human are formed: constructive-destructive, harmonic-disharmonious and so on.

Diagram 5.1.1: Psychical forces form psychical energy

Diagramm OS3-1: Psychische Kräfte formen psychische Energie

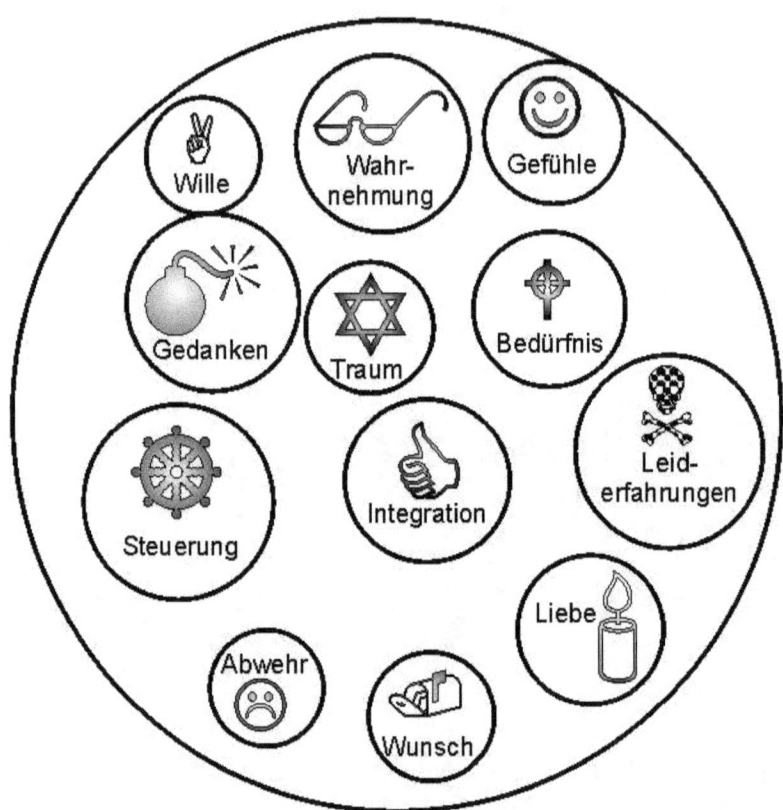

English Translation: Will, perception, emotions, thoughts, dream, needs, control, integration suffering experience, defense, wants, love form in interaction the psychical energy

PSI energy and psychical energy: a fact!

The variety of models about the PSI energy makes it clear that psychical energy is a life phenomenon that cannot be dissuaded away with any positivist science.

Countless parapsychological researches, with many hypotheses, lead to the core problem: In telepathy and clairvoyance, an unknown energetic substance is to be sought.

The consciousness contains one or more new types of energy.

The atmosphere contains an unexplored energy. This energy is present everywhere (orgone energy).

The discovery of the energy associated with psychic processes will be as significant (if not more important) as the discovery of atomic energy. This energy is called "bio-plasmic energy".

'Prana' is another word for "psychical energy," a life force that reveals itself in the universe, but whose place is in the heart of man.

Some talk about aura, ether, or odd energy.

There is an energy field of universal super consciousness.

In transmission, in clairvoyance and telepathy, in mass suggestions and in all kinds of PSI phenomena, "psychical energy" manifests itself.

Consciousness and the unconscious are a unity. They are a single PSI field.

By means of thought experiments one can create PSI fields in space.

Everyone has PSI energy and can use it.

PSI energy is the basis for telepathy and clairvoyance, the energy of the sixth sense.

Extra-sensory perception is a fact that countless people can confirm. ASW can give us an unconscious, gentle guidance in life, and help us make the right decision at the right moment when it is most beneficial to our needs.

Positive thinking and prayer activate a positive PSI energy.

The idea of an energy field and an energy body goes back to ancient times. It is as well-known as by Christianity, and as by Far Eastern philosophers.

The real place of our sensation is not the body, with the brain and the nervous system, but the energy body that is placed over the physical body. This energy body is the superordinate, organizing part of man.

The "energetic soul field" explains telepathy, thought transmission and clairvoyance. Body and soul are two beings.

Model 'Psychic Energetic Body

Abbildung OS3-19: Modell "Psychische Energiekörper "

Von uns erstellt in Anlehnung frei nach Meek G.W.
(Heiler und Heil-Prozess. München 1980, Seiten 235-250)

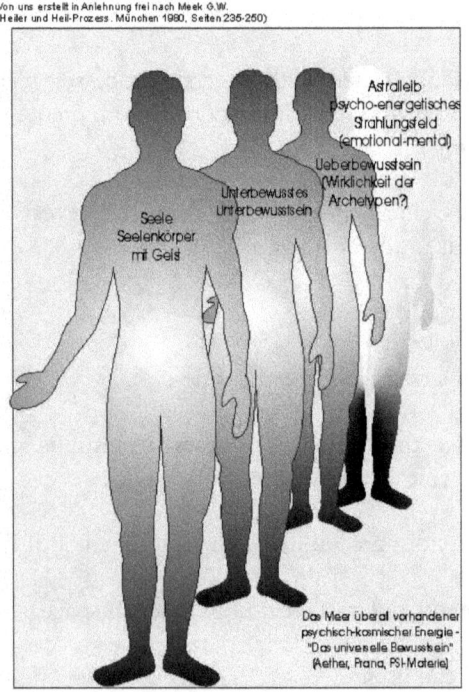

English Translation: Illustration: Model "psychical energy bodies: Constructed by us after: Meek, G.W. (Heiler- und Heilprozess. München1980, Seiten 235-250): Soul, soul body with spirit / Unconscious, unconsciousness / Over consciousness (reality of archetypes?) / Astral body, psycho-energetic radiation field (emotional-mental) act in the sea of everywhere existing psychic-cosmic energy – "The universal consciousness" (ether, prana, PSI-material)

Notes and Perspectives

What can the knowledge about the psychical energy serve?

Write down the key words in this subchapter:

What critical effects can psychical energy have on humans?

Reflecting on PSI powers is essential because:

What did you learn about psychical energy in your parents' home, school, and church?

What meaning- when living together- has the conversation about psychic energy?

To what extent can psychical energy be significant to politics and the economy?

What does advertising convey about the reality of psychic-cosmic energy?

Formulate an important question about psychical energy:

5.1.2. The tensions of psychical energy

A wish is formed. The thoughts are critical. Other needs want to be satisfied first. In addition, there are feelings that want to block the desire to fulfill.

Love pushes for another direction: Abandonment instead doing more for something else. Then a dream about this wish occurs: "It is not good at the moment to fulfill this wish". But the deficit from childhood and adolescence urges: "But I want it now". Such an inner-psychological situation generates a lot of tension.

There are always many psychical powers "in discussion" about what to decide and what to do.

It means: "Unprocessed events from the past gnaws". "Think positive" may well set the accent, because negative thoughts create a tough negative energy over time.

On the other hand, it is almost always difficult to think positively, if the lived life is not cleared, external restrictions on life are threatening, or strokes of fate strike badly.

Every day, the psychical energy is in motion, whether subliminal or visible. Most of the news from the world tends to be hopeless or tragic.

The eye sees a lot of things and the hand would like to hold on. The instruments do not last for the manifoldness. This stresses the experience of psychical energy.

Everyday life activates psychical energy from getting up to falling asleep. Many things are stressing. The reality of life is demanding. The mental life is pressing. How can this be reconciled without overloading?

Many people find no solution to this. They become ill or live a life of depression and powerlessness, hopelessness, and emptiness.

Many experience intense daily pressures on their psychical system: Noise, strangers in the train, neighbors, the boss, the strained marriage, the children, the sick in-laws, the economic crisis, etc.

In addition, comes the entire lived life, which is disordered and unclear to most people. This area also activates the inner life, without even being aware.

One can call this situation 'stress'. Over time, it breaks out of the weak points of the psychic system: psychically, physically, or socially.

It is not the will or the ability to think or the "I" guidance that are the real weak points that 'break' over time or simply no longer have the 'power'.

It is the formed psychical energy that blocks, effects destructively, and makes everything modestly hopeful unreachable.

Reflections and Discussion

The tensions of psychic energy are reflected in:

☐ Nervousness
☐ Pressure on the chest or in the abdomen
☐ Emotional outbursts
☐ Tension headache (migraine)
☐ Palpitations
☐ Sweating
☐ Irregular pulse

Restless, disordered and not centered psychic energy strains:

☐ Vegetative nervous system   ☐ Breathing, circulation, digestion
☐ Concentration   ☐ Responsiveness
☐ Actions   ☐ Mood
☐ Confidence

Mental tension impairs:

☐ Thinking ability
☐ Perception
☐ Handling feelings (e.g. anger)
☐ Forces disposition
☐ Self-control
☐ Learning or open-mindedness
☐ Life options
☐ Vitality
☐ Ability to love
☐ Openness in communication

Chronic excessive mental tensions contain dangers, and can create:

- ☐ Risk of accidents
- ☐ Relationship conflicts
- ☐ Psychosomatic suffering
- ☐ Wrong decision making
- ☐ Crime
- ☐ Irrational behavior
- ☐ Mental disorders
- ☐ Negative living
- ☐ Conflict and violence
- ☐ One-sided thinking
- ☐ Wars

Diagram 5.1.2: Tension of the psychical energy

Diagramm OS3-2: Spannung der psychischen Energie

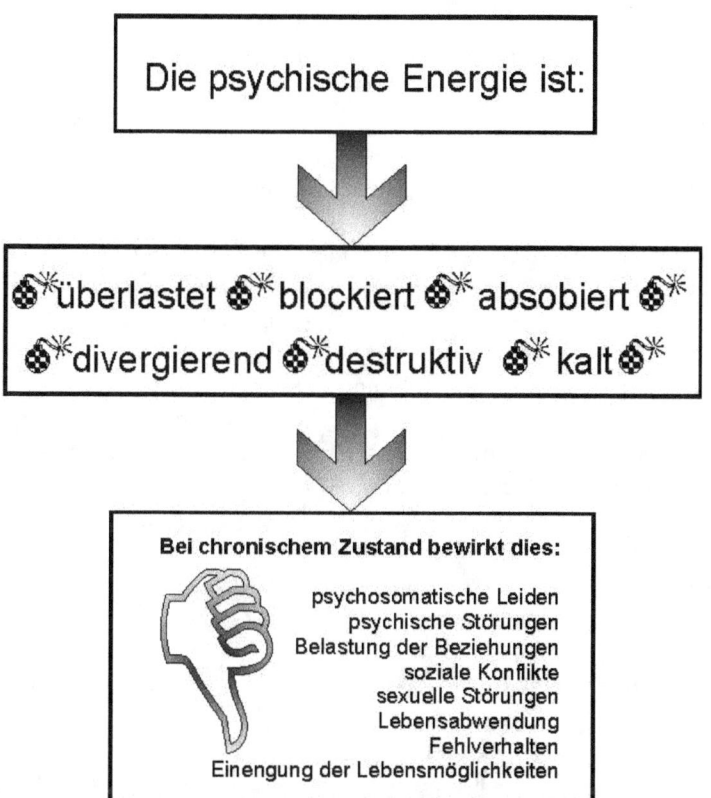

English Translation: The psychical energy is: **overloaded, blocked, absorbed, diverging, destructive, cold** > In a chronic state this effect: Psychosomatic suffering, psychological disturbances, pressure on relations, social conflicts, sexual disorders, avoidance of life, wrongdoing, restriction of life possibilities.

Disturbances of a tense-overstretched state

a) General experience:

- ☐ Tension
- ☐ Inwardly disharmonious
- ☐ Unbalanced mood
- ☐ Negative in terms of mood
- ☐ Not centered in the stomach
- ☐ Not 'rounded'
- ☐ Internally cramped
- ☐ A level of discomfort
- ☐ Inwardly restless
- ☐ Heavy
- ☐ Weak
- ☐ Limp
- ☐ Unbalanced intro- / extravert
- ☐ In bad inner structure
- ☐ Blocked energetically
- ☐ Internally as torn

b) Actual psycho-somatic disorders include:

- ☐ Sleep disorders
- ☐ Migraine, headache
- ☐ Pressure on the chest/in the abdomen
- ☐ Allergies
- ☐ Excessive alcohol consumption
- ☐ Palpitations/heart piercing/heart pressure
- ☐ Blushing
- ☐ Problems with orgasming/life pleasures
- ☐ Menstrual problems
- ☐ Excessive use of painkillers
- ☐ Tension
- ☐ Diarrhea
- ☐ Respiratory symptoms
- ☐ Excessive tobacco consumption
- ☐ Excessive intake of food
- ☐ Excessive sweating
- ☐ Stomach problems
- ☐ Neck pain

c) The reactions to being overloaded, or with negative feelings include:

- ☐ Aggression
- ☐ Being harassed
- ☐ Envy
- ☐ Uncertainty
- ☐ Oppression
- ☐ Worthlessness
- ☐ Despair
- ☐ Inner strife
- ☐ Humiliation
- ☐ Helplessness
- ☐ Depression
- ☐ Mourning
- ☐ Loneliness
- ☐ Injury
- ☐ Failure
- ☐ Rage
- ☐ Boredom
- ☐ Dissatisfaction
- ☐ Weakness
- ☐ Greed
- ☐ Self-estrangement
- ☐ Embarrassment
- ☐ Hopelessness
- ☐ Inferiority
- ☐ Frustrations
- ☐ Rejected
- ☐ Aversion
- ☐ Trouble
- ☐ Lack of Motivation
- ☐ Hate
- ☐ Desolation
- ☐ Scared
- ☐ Listlessness
- ☐ Rejection
- ☐ Discomfort
- ☐ Alienation
- ☐ Emptiness
- ☐ Grief
- ☐ Reluctance
- ☐ Futility

Illustration: Development of the Relaxing State

Abbildung OS3-25: Entwicklung des Entspannungszustandes

Abgezeichnet unter Weglassung der EEG-Angaben aus:
Vaitl, D./Petermann, F.: Handbuch der Entspannungsverfahren.
Band 1. München 1993, Seite 58

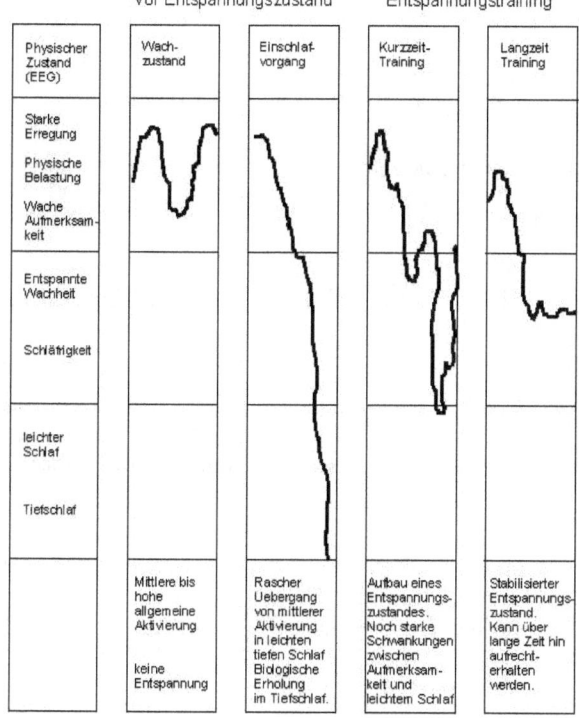

These: Die Störungsanfälligkeit nimmt bei chronischer starker Erregung zu!

English Translation: Drawn without the EEG-indications from: Vaitl, D / Petermann, F.: Handbuch der Entspannungsverfahren. Band 1. München 1993, Seite 58

Thesis: The susceptibility of disturbance arises by chronic strong excitement

Left list: Physical state(EEG): strong excitement, physical pressure, awaken attention / relaxed attention, doziness / slight sleep, deep sleep

Before state of relax: 2. List: Awake state: Middle to high general activation, no relax 3.List: State of falling asleep: Rapid transit from middle activation to slight sleep. Biological recovery in deep sleep.

Relaxing practice: 4. List: Short-time training: Setting of a relaxing state, still big variations between attention and slight sleep. 5. List: Long-time practice: Stable relaxing state can be kept alive a long time.

Notes and Perspectives

What is the benefit of thinking about psycho-energetic tensions?

Write down the key words in this subchapter:

What effects do psycho-energetic tensions have on humans?

Relaxation methods are essential, because:

What have you learned in the home, school, and church about the effects of mental tension?

What significance in living together has the conversation about psycho-energetic tension?

How are the risks of people's psycho-energetic tensions in politics and business reflected?

What does advertising convey about mental tensions?

Formulate an important question about psycho-energetic disorders:

5.1.3. The relaxation of psychical energy

Imagine pictorially a completely relaxed person in a normal everyday situation: with his partner, at work, while cooking, in conversation with the children and so on.

Then you imagine this person in the same situations with total tension of psychic energy. This produces two vastly different pictures.

We all want to experience around us people who are preponderant relaxed. However, we cannot be relaxed around the clock. The psychical life always moves between tension and relaxation.

Tension of the energy is in itself nothing negative. Only with chronic repetition and fixation, can the negative tension become a problem.

Relaxing can be learned. There are various methods for doing this. This includes mental training and other techniques for "psycho hygiene".

Daily relaxation as part of life practice is the answer.

However, a 'nap' after eating hardly allows for relaxation. Nor is having a full stomach for immobilization! Alcohol may relax some people; nevertheless, it can make some more aggressive.

These practices are not really a way. Sunbathing, idling, or lounging about can calm energies. Such practices affect seldom deeply. Many can during hours doing nothing or enjoying the sun without remarkably relaxing.

Hikes or some fresh air during a short walk will reduce tension. Sport can 'discharge' psychical energy and thus be relaxing. Long sleep rarely helps.

This is because the tension of psychical energy does not automatically dissolve with sleep.

Relaxation is a way of life. It is about more than something technical. Part of this way of life is: consider your thoughts, reflect on your feelings, and pay attention to your needs and clarify your unconscious.

Self-determination means e.g.: not absorbing everything, not giving free rein to feelings, paying attention to the external influences and control them (sometimes by avoiding), finding the appropriate day rhythm and always find inner peace in within oneself, and also contemplation.

An inner orientation also contains the reflection on meaning and value.

Self-commitment to love and self-love are both essential.

The integration of dreams, and communication with the "inner spirit" are also essential for a balanced way of life and life development.

If relaxation practices are embedded into a holistic way of life, then the dynamics "tension-relaxation" can become very resilient.

Reflections and Discussion

The relaxation of psychical energy is evident in:

- ☐ Inner peace
- ☐ Forgiveness
- ☐ Perseverance (without compulsion)
- ☐ Serenity
- ☐ Releasing
- ☐ Patience

A Calm, orderly, and centered psychic energy promotes:

- ☐ Self-Strengthening
- ☐ Wellbeing
- ☐ Outer peace
- ☐ Carrying capacity
- ☐ Living settings
- ☐ Health
- ☐ Inner peace
- ☐ Creative performance

Psychological relaxation causes and favors:

- ☐ Centralization
- ☐ Alertness
- ☐ Inner development
- ☐ Constructive behavior
- ☐ Energy balance
- ☐ Concentration
- ☐ Trust

Regular relaxation offers opportunities for:

- ☐ Reduction of disease risks
- ☐ Reduced risk of accidents
- ☐ Promotion of healing processes
- ☐ Building relationships
- ☐ Reduction of susceptibility to interference
- ☐ Focusing on the essentials
- ☐ Alertness to meaning and values
- ☐ Conscious self-education
- ☐ Inner life anchoring

Diagram 5.1.3: Relaxation of the psychical energy

Diagramm OS3-3: Entspannung der psychischen Energie

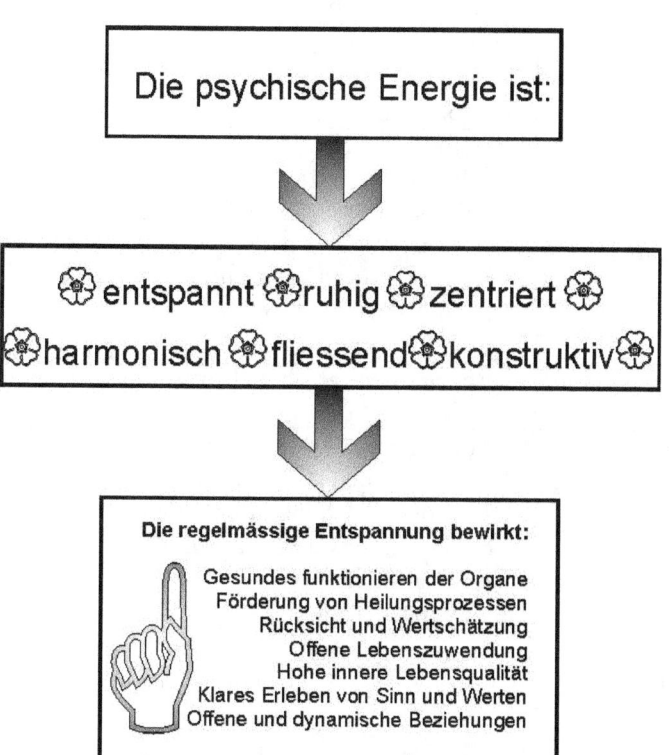

English Translation: The psychical energy is: Relaxed, quiet, centered, harmonic, fluent, constructive > Regular relaxation affects: Healthy functioning of the organs, assistance of healing processes, respect and esteem, open attention for life, high inner quality of life, clear experience of sense and values, open dynamic relations.

The methods and goals of relaxation

The central goals of relaxation processes include:

Relaxing technique	Goals of relaxation
Progressive Muscle Relaxation	☐ Relaxation of the voluntary musculature ☐ General immobilization ☐ Feeling of relaxation ☐ Improve lung function ☐ Improvement of body awareness
Autogenic training	☐ Self-pacification ☐ Self-regulation of involuntary bodily functions ☐ Relaxation of the voluntary musculature ☐ Reduction of sympathetic activity ☐ Regular, slowed breathing
Meditation techniques	☐ Making deep inner peace ☐ Feeling of relaxation ☐ Reduction of activity of the sympathetic nervous system
Imaginative process	☐ Making / changing certain ideas ☐ Change in behavior and experience ☐ Improved handling of emotions
Biofeedback	☐ Self-control over physiological reactions ☐ Body awareness training ☐ General relaxation

Autogenic training, like many other relaxation techniques, allows:

☐ Recreation
☐ Immobilization, compensation
☐ Self-regulation of voluntary body functions
☐ Performance increase (by elimination of disturbances!)
☐ Pain reduction
☐ Emotional balance
☐ Self-education
☐ Self-control (through internal insight)
☐ Self-realization
☐ Reduction of tense living

Autogenic training is not psychotherapy. It does not resolve unconscious complexes and does not process the biography. The state of relaxation achieved by the autogenic training; however, can facilitate a psycho katharsis.

Thesis: Through multiple relaxation methods the brain processes are triggered, which affect the functioning of the organs- both health-preserving and health-promoting processes.

Relaxation in the brain results from:	From solar plexus (through relaxation in the brain) provided organs are:
☐ Positive pictures	☐ Eyes
☐ Constructive thoughts	☐ Salivary gland
☐ Immobilization of thoughts	☐ Containers
☐ Harmonization of the pictures	☐ Heart
☐ Detachable images	☐ Lung
☐ Cognitive distance	☐ Bronchia
☐ Dissolution of opposites	☐ Stomach
☐ Salvation from suffering	☐ Liver
☐ Liberation of conflicts	☐ Intestine
☐ Generation of alpha waves	☐ Kidneys
☐ Mental fitness	☐ Pancreas
☐ Positive body relationship	☐ Bladder
☐ Observe sense reality	☐ Genitals
☐ Acceptance of life	
☐ Live needs with reason	
☐ Be aware in expression of life	
☐ Mindlessness (psycho-hygiene)	
☐ Reduce perception	
☐ Reduce sensory stimuli	
☐ Detachment of space and time	
☐ Deliberate the rhythm of life	
☐ Living health holistically	
☐ Balance rational-intuitive	
☐ Combine analytical and artistic methods	
☐ Integrate logical and spiritual methods	
☐ Network the words of language and pictures	
☐ Think linear and synthetically	

Reference: "Neurale Verbindungen". Vaitl, D./Petermann, F. (Hrgr.): Handbuch der Entspannungsverfahren. Band 1. Weinheim 1993, page 186

Notes and Perspectives

What is the gain of the complex effects of relaxation?

Write down the key words in this subchapter:

What purpose does multiple relaxation methods have for humans?

Reflecting on the disturbances of a tense-spanned state is essential because:

What did you learn about relaxation in your parents' home, school, and church?

What meaning for living together has the conversation about relaxation?

How is psycho-energetic relaxation in politics and business handled?

What does advertising convey about relaxation?

Formulate an important question about relaxation methods:

5.1.4. Exercises

1. How do you physically experience your psychic energy in a weekly review?

2. How do you experience your psychic energy in your perception and thinking?

3. What thoughts and images quickly cause you internal tension?

4. What feelings quickly cause you inner tension?

5. What do you physically experience when you are tense internally?

6. In which situations can you deeply relax?

7. Which external factors quickly activate an internal tension?

8. Energy balance:
8.1. Describe your average general experience:

8.2. Describe your psycho-somatic disorders or susceptibility:

8.3. Describe your average feelings and moods:

8.4. Try to interpret your overall result (causes, meaning) and judge its possible effects.

8.5. Formulate some ideas on what you could do to improve your situation:

9. Relaxation control: Mark what you consciously notice and do:

- [ ] Lock for positive images.
- [ ] Constructive thoughts in everyday life, even for small things.
- [ ] Immobilization of thoughts, daily 2-3x.
- [ ] Harmonization of images through inner imagination.
- [ ] Release liberating images through meditation.
- [ ] Create cognitive distance if thoughts cling too much.
- [ ] Dissolution of opposites through meditative processing.
- [ ] Salvation of suffering through processing.
- [ ] Freedom from conflict through clarification and correct attitude.
- [ ] Practice mental fitness.
- [ ] To maintain a positive body relationship
- [ ] Observe a sense of reality
- [ ] Take life affirmation seriously, even in trivial matters
- [ ] Living needs with reason, balanced, at the right time
- [ ] Consciously direct perception not to 'stroll' too much with the eyes
- [ ] To reduce sensory stimuli: not empathize in everything
- [ ] Detachment of space and time (through meditation)
- [ ] Deliberate rhythm of life, even in hectic professional life
- [ ] Holistic health- mentally and physically
- [ ] A balanced and rational intuition to capture existence
- [ ] Combine analytical artistic methods to manage life concerns
- [ ] Integrated logical spiritual thinking
- [ ] Networking with language and images to capture life
- [ ] Processing linear synthetic (networked thinking)
- [ ] Pay attention to the own biorhythm, especially for specific work
- [ ] Keep internal demarcation to fellow human beings and life topics
- [ ] Create and enjoy pleasure consciously
- [ ] Restrict and control conversation topics

Number of crosses: ...

Formulate your strengths:

Formulate your weaknesses:

How can you strengthen your vulnerabilities?

Multiple Choice Test

Select the four correct answers:

9.1. Psychical energy. Proper statements are:

☐ a) Psychic energy in humans is the electromagnetic energy.
☐ b) Pictorial thoughts come from psychical energy.
☐ c) There is no appreciable psychical energy between people.
☐ d) Images have a stronger psycho-energetic power than thought.
☐ e) Psychical energy can be constructive and / or destructive.
☐ f) Everyone radiates psychic energy.

9.2. The tensions of psychical energy. The following is a direct expression of overly strained psychic energy:

☐ a) Insomnia
☐ b) Migraine
☐ c) Restlessness / nervousness
☐ d) Attention
☐ e) Aggressiveness
☐ f) Indifference

9.3. The relaxation of psychical energy. Relaxed psychical energy generally causes and promotes:

☐ a) Inner satisfaction
☐ b) Good communication
☐ c) Self-confidence
☐ d) Forgiveness
☐ e) Complex resolution
☐ f) Consciousness

5.2. Psycho-Physical Dimensions

5.2.1. The characteristic of psychodynamics

Psychodynamics is the living expression of the formed psychic energy in man. Different terms can have the same meaning., e.g. life energy, vital energy, libido.

Man experiences this energy between tension and relaxation. As vital force expressed itself in someone more outwardly, i.e. extravert, in another more "retired", i.e. introvert. Depending on the state of this vital energy, different psychical and physical reactions occur, e.g. nervousness, cramping, lack of concentration, respiratory pressure, migraine, indigestion and many more.

Whatever the reactions are, everyone experiences their psychodynamics as a basic condition. In one, this experience is more positive, well-adjusted, in another it could be more oppressive or torn.

Stability and lability are a further expression of psychical energy. For some, their energy state will be on-off or unsteady, while others will experience their energy with bigger stableness.

Close to this aspect is the sensitivity of the reactions. In some, the psychical energy system reacts sensitively and flexibly, while in others, the energy is rigid and insensitive. Everyone has his moments where he could "tear up trees". He experiences himself vital, strong, and intense. At other times, the energy is weak, dull, or lame.

Across all aspects of expression, psychical energy acts constructively or destructively according to the state. The energy is one-limiting or liberating, peaceful or aggressive.

Psychical energy is the life energy and thus the psychic life par excellence.

The study of psychodynamics leads to various questions, for example:

☐ What shapes the psycho-energetic state?
☐ How does this energy affect the psychic life, the body, and the action?

☐ How can anyone shape this energy state constructively and revitalize it regularly?

Reflections and Discussion

The characteristics of the individual dimensions are:

- ☐ Tension: restless, unbalanced, disharmonious, uncomfortable
- ☐ Relaxation: calm, balanced, harmonious, comfortable
- ☐ Extraversion: gradual to strongly extroverted
- ☐ Introversion: gradual to highly introverted
- ☐ Psycho-physical reactions: weak to severe susceptibility
- ☐ Basic conditions: from cheerful, lively to gloomy, depressed, sad
- ☐ Stability: firm, stable, steady,
- ☐ Lability: weak, unstable, unsteady
- ☐ Sensitivity: easy to address, flowing, soft
- ☐ Rigidity: rigid, insensitive,
- ☐ Power / intensity: from intense, vital, strong to powerless, weak, lame, dull
- ☐ Constructiveness: inspiring, life-oriented, liberating, peaceful
- ☐ Destructiveness: contagious, lifeless, binding, aggressive

Everyone can profile his psychodynamics using the following pattern:

Tension	Extraversion, Introversion	Psychophysical reactions	Basic condition
Stability, Lability	Sensitivity, Rigidity	Force, Intensity	Constructiveness, Destructiveness

Make notes and discuss comparatively your profile with others in the group. Note that a profile can change and get a new dynamic through education over time.

Diagram 5.2.1: The eight dimensions of psychodynamics

Diagramm OS3-4: Die acht Dimensionen der Psychodynamik

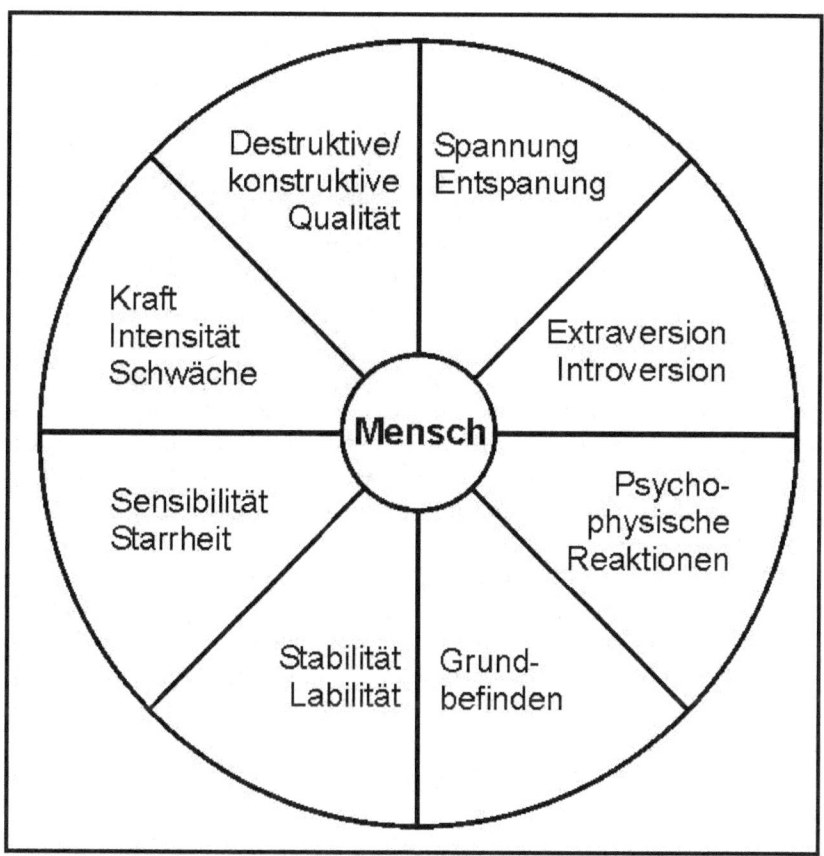

English Translation: A Human's psychodynamic includes: Destructive - constructive quality / Tension – relaxation / Extraversion – introversion / Psychophysical reactions / Basic condition / Stability – lability / Sensitivity – rigidity / Force – intensity -weakness

5.2.2. Psychical energy and its creative power

The psychical energy of a relaxed person is centered and balanced, in itself quiet and calmly flowing, rather light and soft. Within a working environment the person will tense normally, becomes purposeful, and activate a dynamic force in relation to the activity.

The perception will be clear, and the attention focused. The thoughts are steered quietly. The feelings are balanced. The consciousness is active and calm, according to the content as long as we ignore particularly emotional-value-related topics. The inner experience is increasingly active and accessible.

The power of love clearly enters the consciousness. The needs are originally experienced instead of distorted or artificially disfigured. The images in the subconscious are calm, as its energy is relaxed until the subjects are reactivated by daily life. The communication with the spirit, through dreams becomes clear. This condition is especially important in imagination and contemplation.

If the psychic energy is severely tense, uneasy, and torn apart by internal opposing values of thoughts, feelings, and needs, as well as other psychical forces, then the state of stress will be experienced. In extreme cases, especially with chronic tension mental disorders can be the result which psycho-energetic dynamics negatively impact on the entire life.

By relaxing and health-preserving, the relaxed psychical energy influences on the body. Influenced are: Breathing, circulation, digestion, muscles, nerves, sleep, and sexuality. A chronically loaded psychic energy affects also the bodily functions. Many types of disorders and psycho-somatic diseases are the result.

Behavior is also influenced by the state of psychical energy. Man acts differently when he is relaxed, concentrated, or over-strained. The activities of a relaxed person are safe and relieved. The action is moderate, dosed, and considerate. The individual steps of action can be well managed by the "I".

Reflections and Discussion

The relaxed psychic energy:

Soft	Calm	Soothing	Strong
Fluent	Centered	Awake	Bright
Harmonious	Balanced in	Recovered	Equilibrium

	itself		

The overstrained (overly tense) psychic energy:

Hard	Restless	Uncomfortable	Heavy
Rigid	Discordant	Dampening	Stabbing
Blocked	Torn	Cold	Tiring

The psychical energy works according to its condition, and impacts:

☐ All mental functions
☐ The body or organ functions
☐ Action

The experience of psychic functions, of the body and the acting, in all forms of expression of psychical energy has many variations that can differ considerably between people.

Describe your average experience:

Condition of the psychical energy	Reactions in the mental functions	Reactions at the action	Responses in the body and in organ functions
Relaxed psychic energy			
Normal tense psychic energy			
Over-stressed psychic energy			

Discuss your information with others. Compare the variations.

Diagram 5.2.2: The impacts of the psychical energy

Diagramm OS3-5: Die Wirkungen der psychischen Energie

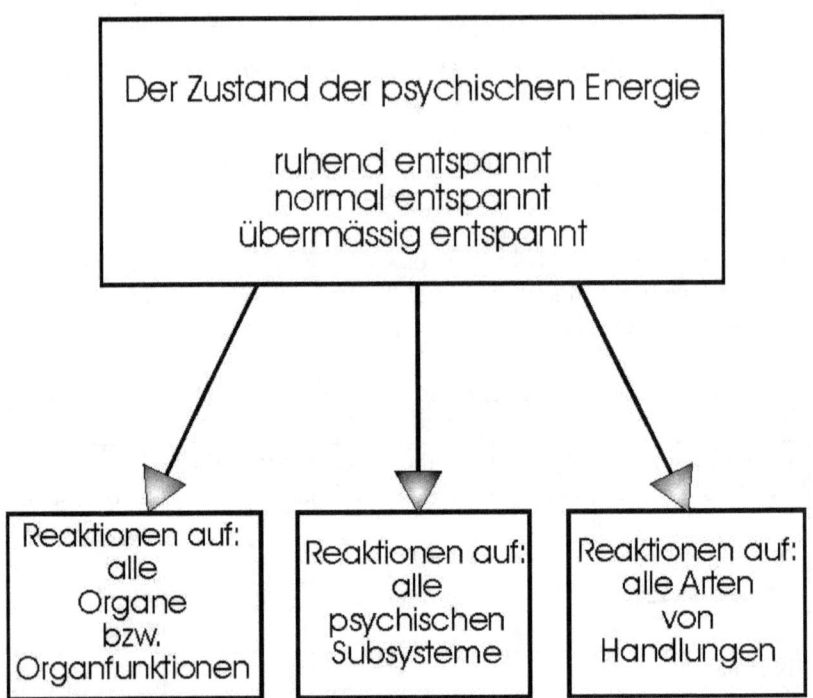

English Translation: The state of the psychical energy: Reposing relaxed, normal relaxed, excessively relaxed > Reactions on: all organs resp. organ functions & > Reaction on all psychical subsystems & > Reactions on all kind of acting.

5.2.3. The emotional causes of tension

Those who pick up insignificant information is unlikely moved by it, e.g. the distance from A to B in a purely factual information. If the person must walk on foot, in rain and the cold and it is some kilometers, it will trigger a feeling of anger and displeasure.

Math-like formulas or numbers barely move people when they see them. For example, if the numbers mean money, depending on the importance of the person in question, it can cause a positive or negative emotional response.

Event situations can be experienced as 'critical' and thus receive an emotional component. Some people who leaf through a holiday brochure may feel excited. In others, the psychic energy stretches because they cannot go on vacation or do not want to go alone.

We assume that the same things and circumstances in people, depending on their subjective meaning, cause quite different experiencing.

Emotions activate psychical energy. All emotional experiencing activates and forms psychical energy inside. We all know these inner effects. The whole range of negative and positive feelings influences thinking and acting, and often impacts on the body.

Feelings of guilt can be experienced inside the body: a 'knot' in the stomach or a tight feeling in the chest. Anger weights on the stomach, everyone knows. Sorrow and worry lead to indigestion. Aggression, anger and, for example, feelings of revenge characterize the acting. The greater the oppression or diffuse fears in life, the more incisive they are to daily actions, and in many cases, to the whole body. Sexual tensions make sick in the long run if they are not otherwise managed.

Many unmet needs cause an experience of emotional frustration, e.g. a lack of tenderness, group affiliation, being accepted, autonomy, work. Thoughts, fantasies, memories, and meditative experiences are also considered as emotional factors if they contain a certain meaning for the person.

Love and hope can trigger strong positive feelings and thus shape the psychic energy accordingly.

Reflections and Discussion

All emotional factors are affective. They contain feelings resp. trigger feelings. Every experiencing with a certain subjective meaning activates feelings that contain meaning and value. We differentiate in a simplified way:

☐ Positive (pleasant) feelings
☐ Negative (unpleasant) feelings

The different types of emotional triggers are:

Critical actions	Thoughts
Events	Insults
Needs	Humiliation
Threats	Bloopers
Noise	Fantasies

The Inventory of the unconscious has a special meaning. Anything that comes into consciousness and addresses image patterns in the unconscious activates them as orientation back bonding or in the sense of the 'unsaved' theme (i.e., complex activation).

Colors, spatial dimensions, and symbols activate psychical energy too, when they become conscious in experiencing.

A weekly review of one's own emotional factors: In the following diagram, write a descriptive keyword that gives a sense and value experience (e.g. a feeling).

Period Weekday	Morning	Late morning	Mid-day	Afternoon	Evening	Night
Monday						
Tuesday						
Wednesday						
Thursday						
Friday						
Saturday						
Sunday						

Diagram 5.2.3: The forces forming the psychical energy

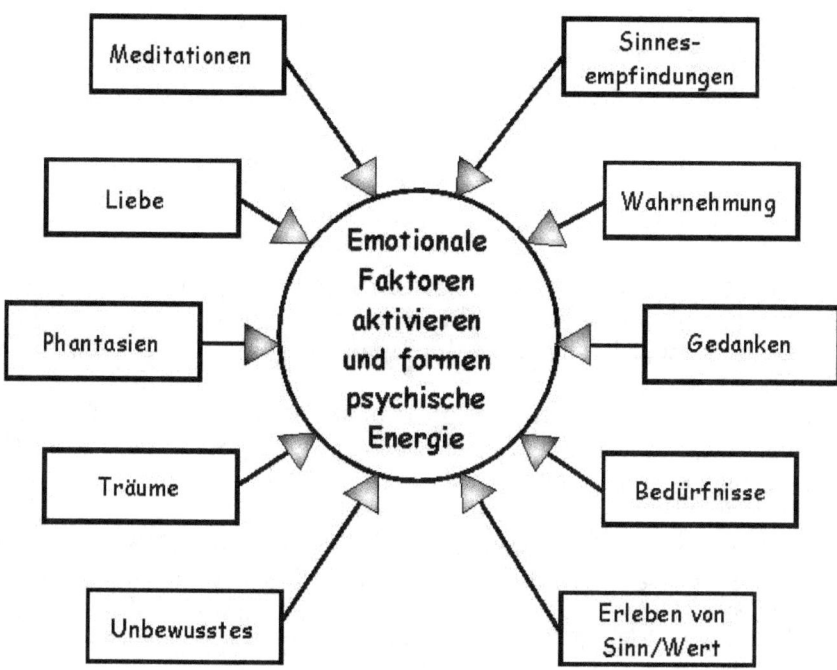

English Translation: Emotional factors activate and shape psychical energy: Experiencing sensations, perception, thoughts, needs, experiencing sense & value, unconsciousness, dreams, phantasies, love, meditations

5.2.4. The tension-generating habitat factors

The psychical energy system- of an individual is influenced by multiple external factors. It is important to be aware that the external reality is only through the internalization, reception in the consciousness, an emotionally effective factor.

There are also sources that act directly as psychic energy on humans. Everywhere in the living space there is formed psychical energy, which we call 'psycho-smog'.

In addition, every human being has a psycho-energetic emission with which he interacts with the people in the direct environment, also telepathically at great distances. In most cases this happens unconsciously and unintentionally.

Furthermore, we assume that there is an intelligent source of power in the universe, something like a "cosmic-energetic sun". Conclusion: All life contains psychic energy and lives from this energy.

The reception of the external reality happens through sensory experience. Colors, shapes, noise levels, fragrances and so on affect human as either pleasant or unpleasant, because they have an objective or subjective significance to him. With the activation ("putting into operation") of the individual psychical subsystems, psychical energy is shaped.

Central are the realities that we have subdivided into life systems. In it we can place the action areas and the reference systems with other people. All these realities affect man through their specific peculiarities.

In addition, many elements have a challenging meaning. Man is urged to act, be it from unspoken rules, be it because of the laws or norms, or because he wants to actively accomplish something in it. The psycho-energetic effect thus comes about in the interaction of human life system (element). In addition, it can be assumed that the individual differences in the existing shaped psychodynamics trigger different reactions.

People psycho-energetically react very differently to the same circumstances, because the meaning varies subjectively and partly because people never have completely identical psychodynamic relations.

Reflections and Discussion

There are various external sources and factors that affect the psychic energy system. These include:

Energy sources	Indirect effects
"Cosmic sun"	Habitats
Energy emission of others	"Critical event situations"
Thought energy of other	Challenging situations
"Psycho-smog"	Interactions

Many external realities have different meanings for humans, and consequently a different energy effect through internalization. Here are a few examples:

Holiday idyll in the mountains	Skiing
Accident report in the newspaper	People praying
Folk music	Refuse on the street
Classical music	Clothes
Motorcycle	Pictures with sexual stimulation
Racing car	Old people
Shopping for food	Sick people

Collect some external impressions from the last few weeks that have made a lasting impact on you.

Describe how you experienced the psychic energy emission of other people and of foreign spaces.

Discuss your experience with others.

Diagram 5.2.4 External effective force on psychodynamics

Diagramm OS3-7: Aeussere Wirkungskräfte auf die Psychodynamik

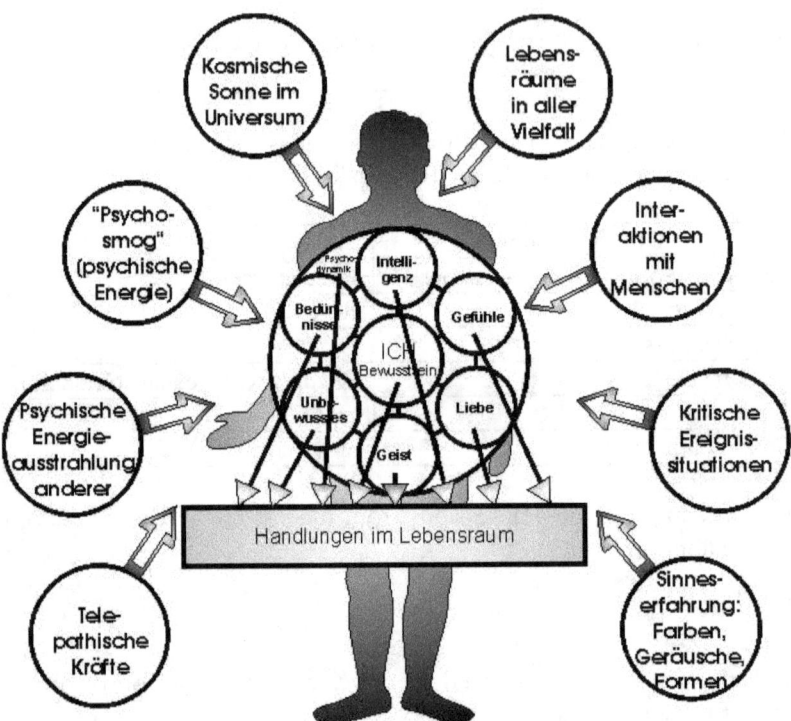

English Translation: Cosmic sun in the universe / Habitats in every diversity / Interactions with humans / Critical event situations / Sensorial experiences: Colors, noise, forms / Telepathic forces / Psychical energy radiation of others / "Psycho-smog" (psychical energy) influence the acting in the habitat and the human with his psychodynamics: Intelligence, needs, feelings, "I" consciousness, unconscious, love, spirit.

5.2.5. The complex stress symptoms

Psychodynamics is the real factor for stress. Imagine the following psycho-energetic situation: The energy is chronically overstretched and excessively extraverted, some psychic forces no longer work normally and / or are more accident-sensitive, firstly evident in a lack of concentration and muscle tension. The basic condition tends to be oppressive and changeable. The energy structure is predominantly discontinuous, and the sensitivity is overactive. In a moment there seems to be a lot of power available, which is then replaced by a 'hole' in the next moment. The energy is aggressive.

What emerges from this in acting is usually a reinforced one-sided reaction patterns of the psychical forces and is increasingly physical, which is referred to 'stress'.

We can thus define 'stress' under different aspects. The first aspect is the location of psychic energy. If a situation, such as our example, weights on the eight dimensions (or some of the eight) for a long time, then this is an expression of stress.

The second aspect relates to the effectiveness of the psychical subsystems. The disruption susceptibility is increasingly evident in various subsystems. Needs are suppressed, feelings are displaced, love is pushed aside, and so on...

Third, somatic reactions show up. These may be in the form of sleeping disorders, , perhaps digestive problems, or migraine.

Fourth, we recognize stress in the actions themselves. The actions become unsteady or increasingly tense. In certain areas the "I" loses control, e.g. during mealtime. Flexibility decreases and the values become increasingly one-sided, e.g. geared to job performance or artificial needs.

There are considerable differences between people in their stress patterns. One may express stress more externally and in hyperactivity. Another person may experience stress internally and be blocked to the outside.

Furthermore, the emotional factors can be located differently, by one in the outer areas, by another in the tense situation due to suppressed psychical subsystems, especially the subconscious and the basic needs.

Reflections and Discussion

Aspects of stress are:

- [ ] The psycho-energetic situation: shaped psychodynamics
- [ ] The functioning of psychical subsystems and their powers
- [ ] The body resp. organ functions and generally somatic reactions
- [ ] The actions in their expression, goal / effect and value

The causes of stress are:

- [ ] In the life systems
- [ ] In the psychical subsystems
- [ ] In the interactions outside-inside

Stress patterns have three main variants:

- [ ] Processes that are primarily directed to the outside
- [ ] Processes that are blocked against the outside and run inside
- [ ] Processes that are predominantly somatically recognizable

If a stressful situation is maintained over a longer period of time, then disturbances in the psychical subsystems, in the somatic area and / or in acting can be expected, which will no longer be rid with simple relaxation techniques.

Stress indexes are:

- [ ] I react very strongly in many circumstances
- [ ] I am depressed when I am not working
- [ ] I have neck / cross tension
- [ ] I am easily disturbed
- [ ] I am nervous
- [ ] I am depressed
- [ ] I have difficulty concentrating
- [ ] I am suddenly disabled / blocked in thinking
- [ ] I have work inhibitions
- [ ] Internally, I am quickly agitated in conflicts
- [ ] I also experience worries physically
- [ ] I cannot switch off at the weekend
- [ ] I have indigestion problems
- [ ] I do a lot of things hastily (eating, dressing, grooming)
- [ ] In the evening, I feel pressured by the daily events

☐ I experience myself pessimistically
☐ I experience everyday life as hectic
☐ I am easy to upset
☐ I am impatient
☐ I am hot tempered

Talk about stress and stress reactions in the group.

Diagram 5.2.5: Structure model of stress causes

Diagramm OS3-8: Strukturmodell der Stressursachen

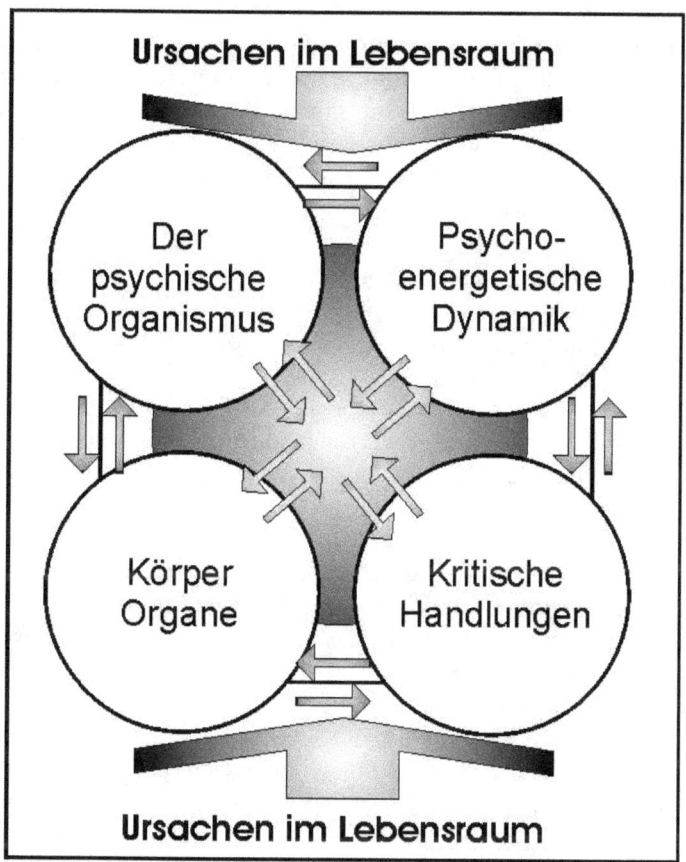

English Translation: Causes in the habitat interact with: The psychical organism & Psych-energetic Dynamic & Body organs & Critical event situations.

5.2.6. Methods of relaxation

With relaxation techniques we can balance, center and strengthen the psychodynamics. Relaxation generally affects all dimensions of psychodynamics. With a relaxation technique, however, the individual psychic subsystems cannot be changed. It does not correct images in the unconscious or build the power of love. Also, you do not train thinking, nor cleaning your feelings.

Relaxation techniques do not clarify or cure neither neurosis nor disorders of mental functions. The goal of relaxation is to find the situation of psychic energy, i.e., the psychodynamics and its effects on body and acting.

With the methods of relaxation, you can create favorable conditions for the formation of personality, lifestyle, and health. In a relaxed state, one sees the realities of life more clearly, is in some situations more deliberate and creates life more balanced. Those who are relaxed learn more easily and are more open to self-reflection. In a relaxed state, one senses the real needs more directly and is more responsive to the power of love.

With regular relaxation, inner stability is built up, a balance between extraversion and introversion is found, and you experience yourself self-centered and 'completely'. If you are relaxed, you are more open to inner experiences.

Thus, relaxation is also a prerequisite for meditation and concentrated work on the inner forces, especially the unconscious inventory. Relaxation also releases new energy.

However, relaxation alone does not create a wise person, nor a life rooted in individuation. Practicing relaxation techniques is a form of psycho hygiene. As one regularly cultivates the body, cleans the living space, washes clothes and arranges things, so the relaxation technique is a method that belongs to the daily life for "internal ordering of the forces".

Indirectly it promotes the functioning of psychical powers, such as: concentration, memory, willpower, self-control and more.

Reflections and Discussion

We focus here on verbal procedures and especially on autogenic training. There are various relaxation techniques. These include:

- Verbal-suggestive (auto suggestive) methods
- Mental training
- Progressive muscle relaxation

Verbal-suggestive relaxation techniques are based on:

- Every mental idea forms psychical energy, the psychodynamic.
- Every inner picture forms psychical energy. This results in a "psycho-physical switching".
- The effect of ideas and images are meaningful (e.g. the sun causes warmth, blue causes calm and so on.).
- The change in the psycho-energetic situation affects the body resp. the organs (circulation, muscles, respiration, etc.).
- The change in the psycho-energetic situation affects the psychical subsystems, with their individual forces.
- The change in the psycho-energetic situation affects the action.

Exercise and application:

Relaxation techniques should first be practiced daily in small steps. Anyone who has practiced a relaxation technique can use it daily in some small moments for a few minutes with a good effect. The psycho-physical switching is fast and direct.

Autogenic training is the classic verbal-suggestive relaxation technique that can be practiced step by step every day. Practice the autogenic training according to the diagram. In a group, this technique is easier to learn. It is sufficient if you perform an exercise every day for ten minutes (lying or sitting). Write down the result afterwards.

The mental training is active imagination, e.g. "emptying head". For this, sit on a chair, slightly tilted forward. Close your eyes and imagine that you have a "spiritual hole" at the forehead. Now all the thoughts, perceptions (things, people, etc.) of the last hours and days fall out of this hole into a bowl. Imagine that thoughts and ideas come out of there until the head is empty.

Diagram 5.2.6: Practice Steps of Autogenic Training

Exercise 1: Heaviness
Right arm heavy. Left arm heavy. Arms heavy. 6x
Right leg warm. Left leg warm. Legs warm. 6x
I am completely quiet. 1x

Exercise 2: Warmth
Right arm warm. Left arm warm. Arms warm. 6x
Right leg warm. Left leg warm. Legs warm 6x
I am completely quiet. 1x

Exercise 3: Heart
Heart pulse quiet and forceful. 6x
Heart pulse regularly. 6x
Heart pulse forceful. 6x
I am completely quiet. 1x

Exercise 4: Respiration
It breathes quit. 6x
Body breaths quiet. 6x
I am completely quiet. 1x

Exercise 5: Solar plexus (stomach)
Solar plexus fluent warm. 6x
I am completely quiet. 6x

Exercise 6: Forehead-Head
Forehead slightly cool. 6x
Forehead slightly fresh. 6x
I am completely quiet. 1x

Procedure:
Week 1: Exercise 1
Week 2: Exercise 1 + 2
Week 3: Exercise 1+2+3
Week 4: Exercise 1+2+3+4
Week 5: Exercise 1+2+3+4+5
Week 6: Exercise 1+2+3+4+5+6

Close of the exercise: "1, 2, 3. bending and stretching arms. 3 times breathing deeply. Open eyes.

5.2.7. Working unit

5.2.7. Working unit - 1

1. a) How do you experience your psychodynamics in your life?

1. b) Extend this topic with your own discoveries:

2. a) Create your profile of your psychodynamics for:

Tension	Extraversion, Introversion	Psychophysical reactions	Basic condition
Stability, Lability	Sensitivity, Rigidity	Force, Intensity	Constructiveness, Destructiveness

2. b) Interpret the causes, meaning, effects, etc:

3. Formulate an educational goal about your psychodynamics:

4. a) Imagine the characteristic of your psychodynamics:

4. b) Your conclusion in one sentence:

5.2.7. Working unit - 2

1. a) How do you experience your tension and relaxation in daily life?

1. b) Expand this topic with your own experience:

2. Describe your average experience for the reactions:

Condition of psychic energy	Reactions in the mental functions	Reactions in the acting	Responses in the body and in organ functions
Relaxed psychical energy			
Normal tense psychical energy			
Over-stressed Psychical energy			

3. Formulate an educational goal in the context of your reaction patterns:

4. a) Imagine your tension-relaxation:

4. b) Your conclusion in one sentence:

5.2.7. Working unit - 3

1. a) What emotional factors do you experience especially in your life?

1. b) Expand this topic with your own experience:

2. a) Consider your own emotional factors in this weekly review: Note in the individual fields of the following diagram a keyword that was a sense and value experience (i.e., a feeling).

Period Weekday	Morning	Late morning	Mid-day	Afternoon	Evening	Night
Monday						
Tuesday						
Wednesday						
Thursday						
Friday						
Saturday						
Sunday						

2. b) Interpret your overall impression:

3. Formulate an educational goal in the context of the emotional factors:

4. a) Imagine an emotional factor that is important to you:

4. b) Your conclusion in one sentence:

5.2.7. Working unit - 4

1. a) How do you experience the effect of external factors on your energy?

1. b) Extend the powers of action with some combinations:

2. a) Collect from the last few weeks some external impressions that have sustained you:

2. b) Describe how you have experienced the psychic energy emission of other people and of foreign areas:

2. c) How can you protect yourself from external impressions and external emanations? Give some tips:

3. Formulate an educational goal for you about the stress-inducing factors:

4. a) Think about external factors that have particularly moved you:

4. b) Your conclusion in one sentence:

5.2.7. Working unit - 5

1. a) How do you experience stress in your life?

1. b) Extend this topic by considering stress in others:

2. Stress indexes are (check what applies to you):

6 = complete; 5 = very; 4 = predominantly; 3 = medium; 2 = partial; 1 = little; 0 = not

☐ I react very strongly in many circumstances
☐ I am depressed when I am not working
☐ I have neck / shoulder tension
☐ I am easily disturbed
☐ I am nervous
☐ I am depressed
☐ I have difficulty concentrating
☐ I am quickly disabled / blocked in thinking
☐ I have work inhibitions
☐ I am quickly agitated in conflicts internally
☐ I also experience worries physically
☐ I cannot switch off at the weekend
☐ I have indigestion problems
☐ I do a lot of things hastily (eating, dressing, grooming)
☐ In the evening, I am pressured by the daily events
☐ I experience myself pessimistically
☐ I experience hectic everyday life
☐ I'm easy to upset
☐ I am impatient
☐ I am fast tempered

Write down your total score here: ....

Interpret:

3. Formulate an educational goal for your stress reactions:

4. a) Imagine your stress:

4. b) Your conclusion in one sentence:

5.2.7. Working unit - 6

1. a) What are your experiences with relaxation techniques?

1. b) Expand the spectrum of effects of relaxation:

2. a) My difficulties with autogenic training are:

2. b) My difficulties with mental training are:

2. c) Relaxation training causes in my life:

2. d) Interpret 2. a) and 2. b):

3. Formulate an educational goal for relaxation exercises:

4. a) Imaginate your difficulties to relax:

4. b) Your conclusion in one sentence:

5.2.7. Work unit - 7

Write an ironic short story: It is to over the period of a month, and about all the people in city, and how they are incredibly stressed!

Multiple Choice Test

Select the four correct answers:

10.1. Characteristics of psychodynamics are:
☐ a) Tension
☐ b) Extra- / Introversion
☐ c) Stability / Lability
☐ d) Cycle
☐ e) Psycho-physical reactions
☐ f) Spiral process

10.2. Psychic energy acts on:

☐ a) Clothes
☐ b) Psychical forces
☐ c) Body functions
☐ d) Actions
☐ e) Plant life
☐ f) Material energy sources

10.3. Which of the following sentences are correct?

☐ a) Embarrassing situations cause emotional impulses.
☐ b) Images-fantasies activate emotions.
☐ c) Situations with threats are "emotional triggers".
☐ d) Long viewing geometric figures can cause tensions through emotion.
☐ e) Noise triggers emotions, especially continuous noise.
☐ f) Impersonal factual information has a subliminal emotive effect.

10.4. The psychical energy system is directly affected by:

☐ a) Smog
☐ b) Psychical energy of others
☐ c) Room impregnation
☐ d) Telepathy
☐ e) Every thought of others
☐ f) The collective unconscious

10.5. Aspects of stress reactions are:

☐ a) Somatic reaction
☐ b) Disruption of a mental function
☐ c) Pressure to act
☐ d) Addiction
☐ e) Inhibition of the drives
☐ f) Internal arousal

10.6. Classic relaxation techniques are:

☐ a) Autogenic training
☐ b) Neo-Analytical Psychotherapy
☐ c) Hypnosis with / without suggestion
☐ d) Mental training
☐ e) Progressive muscle relaxation
☐ f) Walks